XIII thirteen

OFFICIAL STRATEGY GUIDE

by Philip Hansen & Christian Sumner

XIII™ OFFICIAL STRATEGY GUIDE

BradyGAMES®

An Imprint of Pearson Education
800 East 96th Street, 3FL
Indianapolis, Indiana 46240

ISBN: 0-7440-0241-9

Library of Congress No.: 2003112407

Printing Code: The rightmost double-digit number is the year of the book's printing; the rightmost single-digit number is the number of the book's printing. For example, 03-1 shows that the first printing of the book occurred in 2003.

06 05 04 03 4 3 2 1

Manufactured in the United States of America.

BRADYGAMES STAFF

Publisher
DAVID WAYBRIGHT
Editor-In-Chief
H. LEIGH DAVIS
Marketing Manager
JANET ESHENOUR
Creative Director
ROBIN LASEK
Licensing Manager
MIKE DEGLER
Assistant Marketing Manager
SUSIE NIEMAN

CREDITS

Senior Development Editor
DAVID B. BARTLEY
Screenshot Editor
MICHAEL OWEN
Book Designer
DOUG WILKINS
Production Designer
BOB KLUNDER

CONTENTS

INTRODUCTION

The President of the United States of America has been assassinated.

You wake up on a desolate strip of New England beach. The near-fatal impact of a bullet has left your head pounding, and your memory erased. What's more, the number "XIII" has been mysteriously tattooed on your chest, while your pocket holds a key to a New York City bank box. Head swimming in amnesia, you struggle to your feet only to encounter more assailants intent on finishing the job. To your shock, you handle the hitmen with the killing skills of a professional—before heading to the bank in search of any shred of information about your lost identity and your involvement in the President's murder.

What lies ahead is a deadly quest not only into your shadowy past, but also America's darkest corridors of power...

HISTORY OF LUCKY XIII

Here is what we know:

A man wakes up on a beach. He has no recollection of who he is.

He sets off in search of his past. His only clues are the number "XIII" tattooed on his collarbone and the key to a safety-deposit box in one of New York's most prestigious banks.

The passport he finds in the safe at the bank reveals his identity. His name is Steve Rowland and he's a captain in the United States Army. Moments after making this discovery, he's arrested by Colonel Amos, director of the FBI's anti-terrorist department. He's accused of the murder of William Sheridan, the 43rd president of the United States. As evidence, he's shown the enlargement of a snapshot in which he appears holding a sniper's rifle. The weapon is aimed at the presidential cortège. Despite this exhibit, in his heart of hearts he knows he's no murderer. All the same, when killers try to eliminate him, he is surprised to find he has the reflexes of an elite commando.

Wanted by all the cops in New York State and hunted down by The Mongoose, the amnesiac seems doomed to a choice of death or prison. But XIII hasn't counted on the unexpected assistance of Major Jones, a young female soldier who helps him flee through the city of New York. During their escape, this foxy lady reveals to XIII that he's a secret agent working for General Carrington. Carrington is a nonconformist officer who was conducting a counter-inquiry into the presidential assassination when he was arrested and confined in an isolated military base in the Appalachian Mountains.

When XIII realizes that General Carrington is the only one who can shed light on his past, he sets off to find him with Jones.

THE BASICS OF XIII

GETTING STARTED

Since you have lost your memory, XIII, you might need a little help getting around in the game. Here's a brief checklist to get you started.

- Read the game manual. Basic gameplay facts and information on multiplayer can be found in your game manual. A manual is what you have instead of a memory, XIII.
- Visit the Ubisoft website at http://www.ubi.com for information on other Ubisoft game products, and to play the PC CD-ROM version of XIII online.
- Visit the official XIII homepage at http://www.whoisXIII.com for game trailers, screenshots, background information, and a forum where you can communicate with other agents caught up in the conspiracy surrounding XIII.
- Visit the official XIII community page at http://www.whoisXIII.com/community for the most late-breaking news on the game, game reviews, and links to behind the scenes articles.
- Take your game further. When your mission is complete, pick up other fine strategy guide products at http://www.bradygames.com.

CONSOLE CONTROLS

Since you have lost your memory, XIII, you might need a little help getting around in the game. Here's a brief checklist to get you started.

GAMECUBE

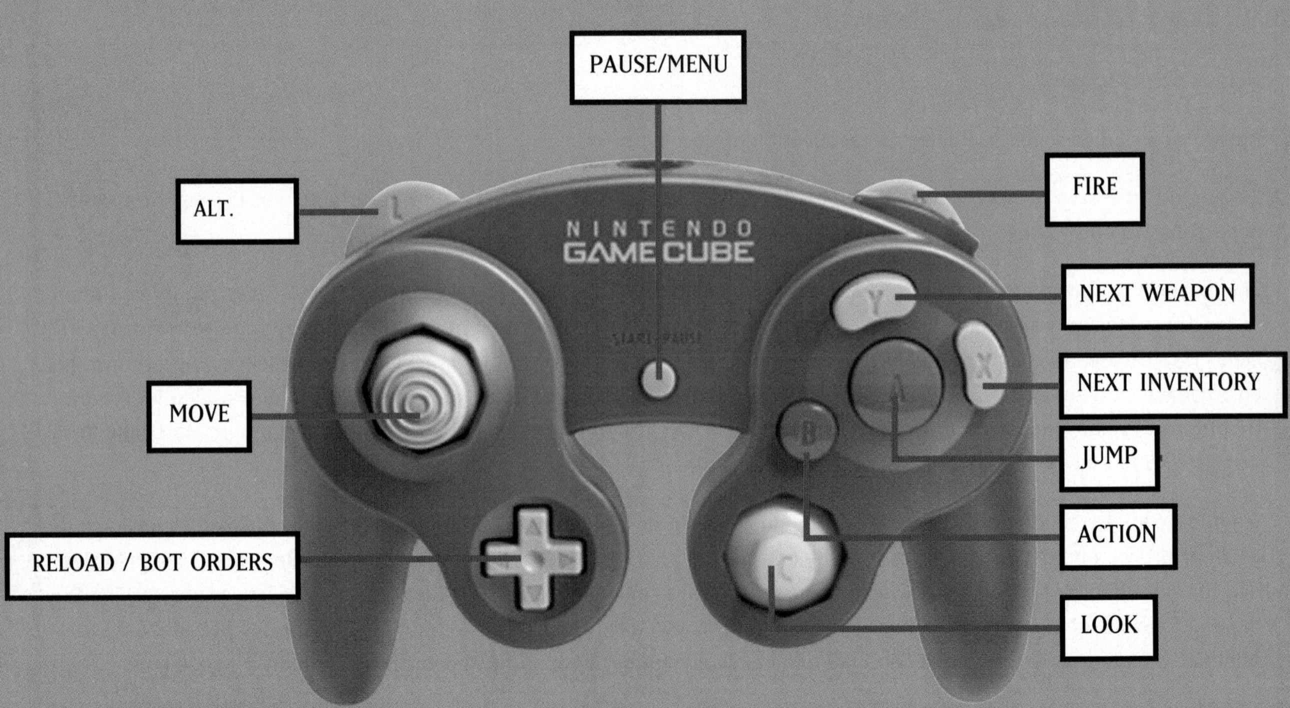

PLAYSTATION 2

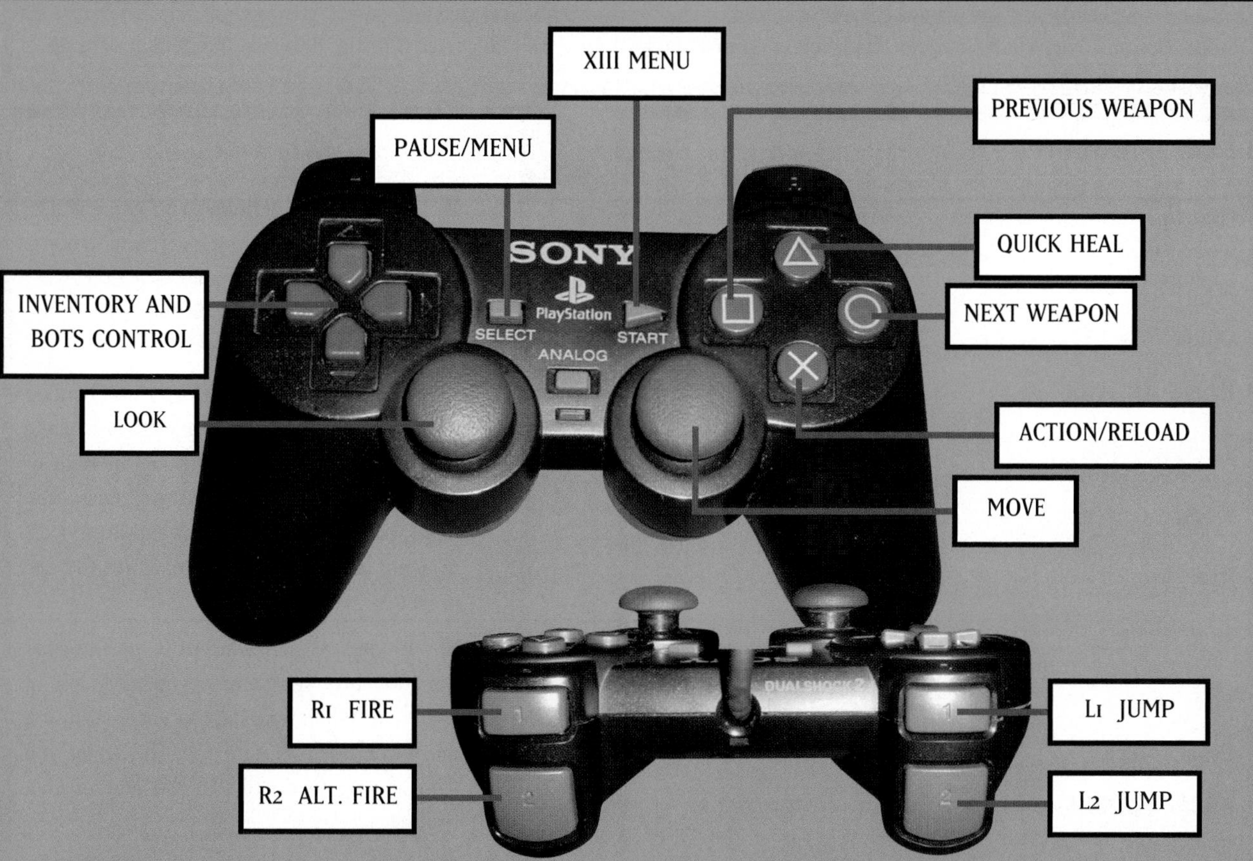

XBOX

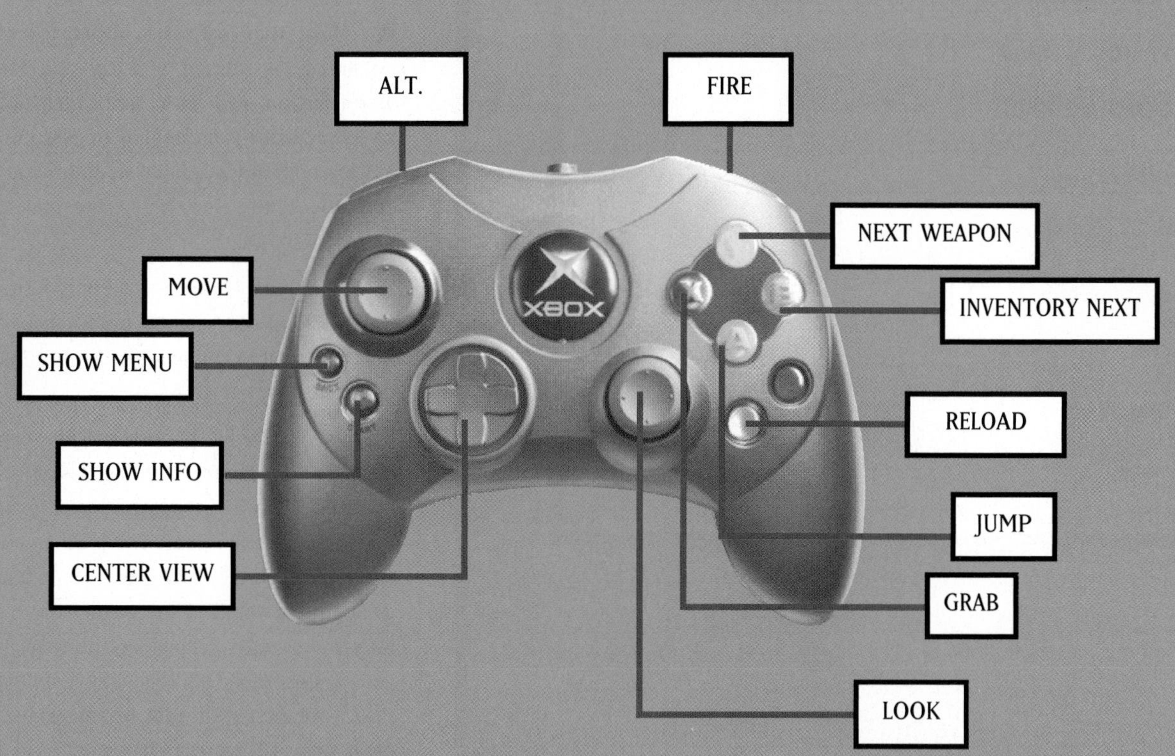

PC CONTROLS

Select Options from the Main menu, then select Controls to customize the PC game controls. Here are the default settings:

Look Options

Look Up	Backspace
Look Down	=
Center View	End

Move Options

Forward	Rightmouse or Z
Backward	Down or S
Strafe Left	Left or Q
Strafe Right	Right or D
Up/Jump	Space or Up
Down/Crouch	CTRL or C

Shoot Options

Attack	Leftmouse
Alt. Fire	Middlemouse
Reload	R
Next Weapon	PageUp or X
Previous Weapon	PageDown or W

Other Options

Grab / Use	Enter or Delete
Prev Inventory	G or Numpad1
Next Inventory	F or Numpad0
Chat	T
Chat Team	Y
Pause	Pause

XIII GENERAL TIPS

- **Don't harm civilians.** You know you're not a killer, XIII, so don't start now. When a civilian or law enforcement officer gets in your way, use a chair, bottle, ashtray, or broom to knock them out.
- **Hide the bodies.** With any one-handed weapon equipped (9mm, MiniGun, Throwing Knife, 44 Special) you can pick up the body of a dead or unconscious enemy. Carry the body some place out of sight and drop it off to avoid alerting patrolling enemies to your presence.
- **Reload.** Watch your HUD for information on how much ammo you have left in each clip. When you start to get low, find a place to hide and hit Reload. This keeps you from having to do this in the middle of a firefight.
- **Silence is golden**. The Throwing Knives, Crossbow, Silenced 9mm, and blunt weapons (chair, bottle, ashtray, broom) are all silent or nearly silent. Use them to quietly eliminate an enemy when there are other foes in the area.
- **Make that last ditch effort.** If you see an enemy is alerted and running for an alarm button, run after him! Catch up and knock him out from behind or just kill him quickly with any available weapon. You may still have time to do this before that alarm button is sounded.
- **Heal with MedKits.** You only have one life, XIII, so keep yourself in top shape with the MedKits and Full MedKits you find out in the field.
- **Use hostages.** A hostage can serve as cover when you are outnumbered and surrounded. Move slowly toward your enemies and they will back away. You have an advantage, XIII—you can still equip a one-handed weapon and shoot at the enemy while gripping a hostage. Remember, however, that you cannot reload while you have a hostage. Pick a weapon with a lot of ammo, like the 9mm, or use Throwing Knives.

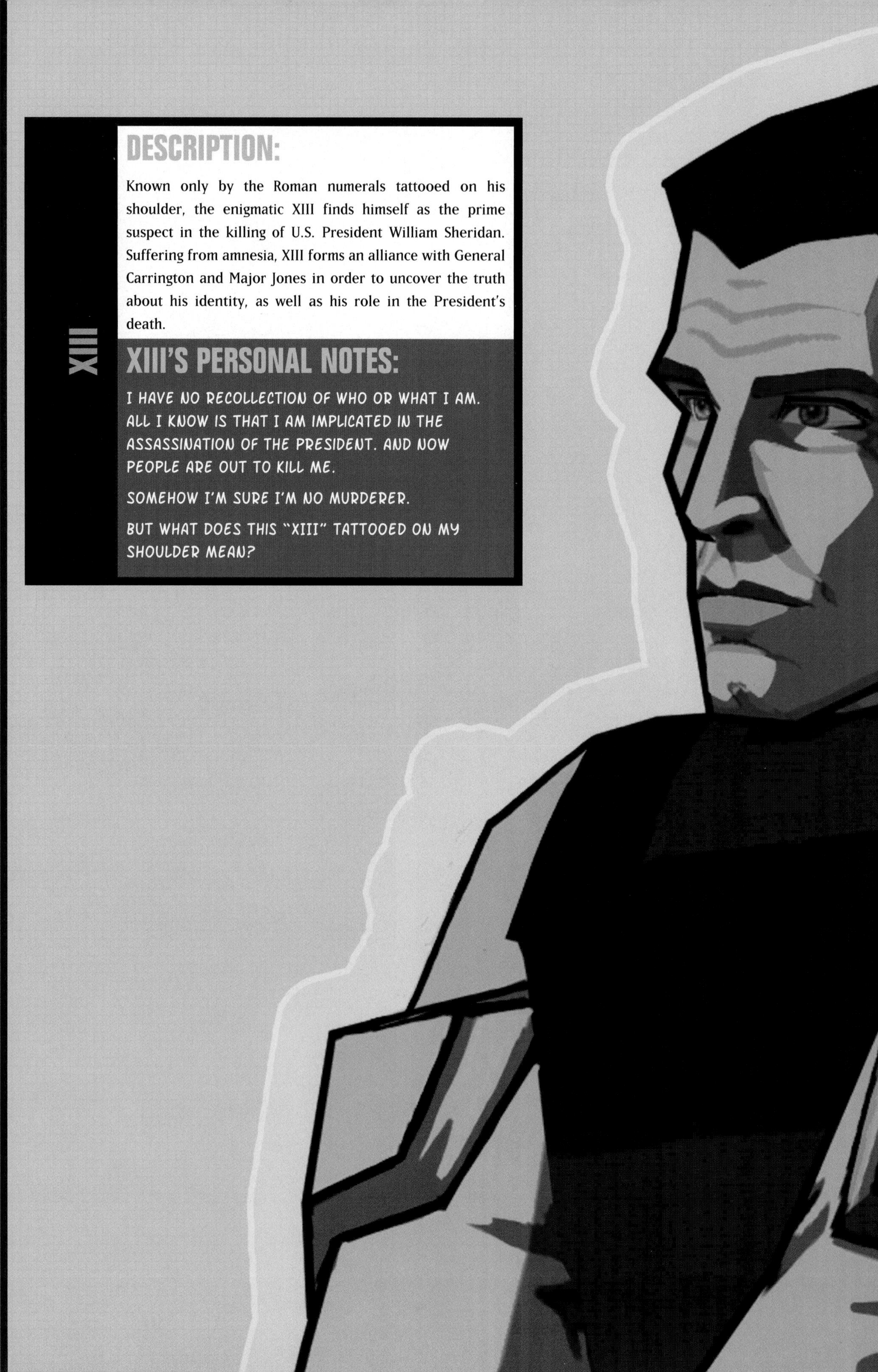

XIII

DESCRIPTION:

Known only by the Roman numerals tattooed on his shoulder, the enigmatic XIII finds himself as the prime suspect in the killing of U.S. President William Sheridan. Suffering from amnesia, XIII forms an alliance with General Carrington and Major Jones in order to uncover the truth about his identity, as well as his role in the President's death.

XIII'S PERSONAL NOTES:

I HAVE NO RECOLLECTION OF WHO OR WHAT I AM. ALL I KNOW IS THAT I AM IMPLICATED IN THE ASSASSINATION OF THE PRESIDENT. AND NOW PEOPLE ARE OUT TO KILL ME.

SOMEHOW I'M SURE I'M NO MURDERER.

BUT WHAT DOES THIS "XIII" TATTOOED ON MY SHOULDER MEAN?

GENERAL CARRINGTON

DESCRIPTION:

The Interservice Chief of Staff at the Pentagon, Carrington is a decorated war veteran and a firebrand within the military community. When William Sheridan was assassinated, he decided to conduct his own, unauthorized investigation to hunt down the killer—a bold move which landed him in a military stockade.

XIII'S PERSONAL NOTES:

INTERSERVICE CHIEF OF STAFF–HIGHEST U.S. MILITARY POST.

CONDUCTING HIS OWN INQUIRY INTO THE ASSASSINATION. UNCONVENTIONAL, BUT A GOOD SOURCE OF INFORMATION AND A GOOD MAN.

SHORT-TEMPERED.

Characters

GENERAL CARRINGTON

MAJOR JONES

DESCRIPTION:

General Carrington's protégé and confidential assistant, the talented Major Jones is at once a deadly beauty and crack Air Force test pilot. Jones' latest assignment is to aid, inform, and protect XIII as he infiltrates the corrupt power structure of the U.S. government. Beyond these duties, Jones hides a secret motive for helping XIII.

XIII'S PERSONAL NOTES:

ASSISTS GENERAL BEN CARRINGTON IN INVESTIGATING THE CONSPIRACY BEHIND THE PRESIDENT'S ASSASSINATION.

COLONEL AMOS

DESCRIPTION:

A veteran commando from the first Arab-Israeli war. Now, as the director of the FBI's anti-terrorist initiative, Colonel Amos leads the official inquiry into the President's death. He wages an all-out hunt for XIII after he discovers an amateur film of the assassination, and positively identifies XIII as the trigger man.

XIII'S PERSONAL NOTES:

RUNNING THE OFFICIAL FBI ENQUIRY INTO THE DEATH OF PRESIDENT SHERIDAN.

VERY METHODICAL AND INTELLIGENT, BUT LACKS GUT-INSTINCT.

LOYAL ONCE HIS TRUST HAS BEEN EARNED.

WALLY SHERIDAN

DESCRIPTION:

The impassioned brother of assassinated president William Sheridan. In a moving speech, Wally announced his mission to continue in his brother's footsteps as the leader of the free world. A member of the budget commission in Congress, Sheridan uses his status to help XIII penetrate high-security areas.

XIII'S PERSONAL NOTES:

IS HELPING GENERAL CARRINGTON CARRY OUT HIS INQUIRY INTO THE ASSASSINATION OF HIS BROTHER, WILLIAM. HAS PROMISED TO STAND AGAINST THE REPUBLICAN CANDIDATE JOSEPH K. GALBRAIN.

A NOTORIOUS CHARMER.

THE MONGOOSE

DESCRIPTION:

A feared hitman operating under orders from the shadow organization known as "The Twenty"—the same elusive group whom General Carrington suspects as the engineers behind the President's death. The Mongoose commands an army of henchmen, with one mission: eliminate XIII at all costs.

XIII'S PERSONAL NOTES:

SEEMS TO BE INVOLVED IN THE PRESIDENTS DEATH. A DARK, SHADOWY CHARACTER WITH THE DEMEANOR AND SKILLS OF A PROFESSIONAL KILLER WHO IS NOT USED TO FAILURE.

HE WANTS ME **DEAD**.

KIM ROWLAND

DESCRIPTION:

An unlikely spy, Kim Rowland was recruited from a college campus by CIA scouts at the age of 22. After a handful of training sessions, she became a sleeper agent for three years. Kim was activated by Carrington after he confirmed the existence of the shadow organization, "The Twenty."

XIII'S PERSONAL NOTES:

SHE DISAPPEARED WHILE INVESTIGATING THE CONSPIRACY BEHIND THE MURDER OF THE PRESIDENT. WAS WORKING WITH GENERAL CARRINGTON.

COLONEL MacCALL

DESCRIPTION:

An obsessive hard-core military commander who follows orders without question. This is General Standwell's right-hand man and where Standwell leads, MacCall will follow.

XIII'S PERSONAL NOTES:

RUNS THE SPADS (SPECIAL ASSAULT DESTROYING SECTION) CAMP ON AN ISLAND OFF THE MEXICAN COAST.

GENERAL STANDWELL

DESCRIPTION:

Power hungry and politically ambitious, William S. Standwell is the driving force behind the elite SPADS military unit. The question is, whose side are the SPADS on? The country's or General Standwell's?

XIII'S PERSONAL NOTES:

HARDLINE POLITICAL FIGURE WHO DREAMS OF REPLACING GENERAL CARRINGTON AS MILITARY CHIEF OF STAFF.

FIERY TEMPER.

EQUIPMENT DATABASE

WEAPONS

KNIFE

DESCRIPTION:

The Knife is an ideal weapon for close-quarters combat, and can also be hurled at enemies. Be careful, though—the further you throw, the less accurate this weapon becomes.

ARMORY NOTES:

When silence is required, the Knife is your best bet. Get in close to a enemy and score a headshot with a Throwing Knife for a quick kill.

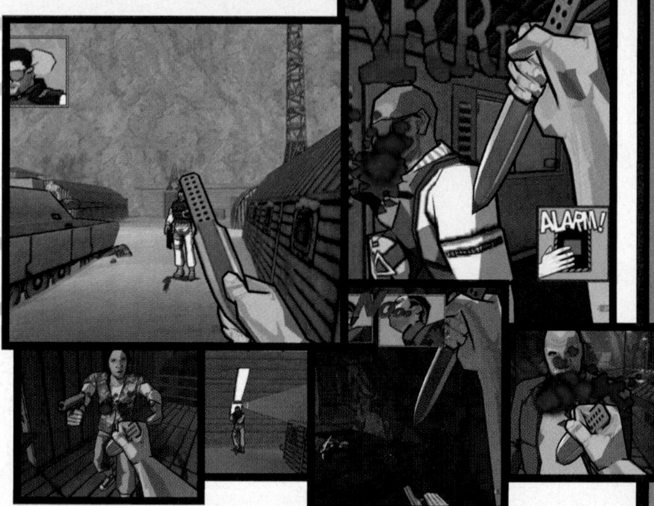

9MM HANDGUN

DESCRIPTION:

The Handgun can unload 13 bullets before you need to reload. If the task at hand requires a little stealth, screw on the silencer. And for situations when sneaking around is totally out of the question and a single gun just isn't enough, pick up a second and use one in each hand.

ARMORY NOTES:

The 9mm can be equipped with a silencer for some quiet kills. The drawback here is that this is not a "one-shot, one-kill" weapon. It takes two or three hits to put an enemy down with the 9mm.

44 SPECIAL

DESCRIPTION:

Dirty Harry's favorite is a ruthlessly effective weapon over short-to-middling distances. It holds six bullets, but if you're in trouble it's possible to empty the whole lot in one go.

ARMORY NOTES:

Power and decent range combine in a single package with the 44 Special. Use it to score "one-shot, one-kill" head shots on any enemy without a helmet. If you're feeling lucky, the 44 Special is a reliable choice.

HUNTING GUN

DESCRIPTION:

While the Hunting Gun's wide shot-scatter makes it a deadly weapon over short distances, it's less effective at long range. You must reload after firing just two shots, but you can always use the butt to smack your opponents if you're in a tight spot.

ARMORY NOTES:

With only two shells and a slow reloading time, the Hunting Gun is a poor substitute for the regular Shotgun. This is essentially a weapon of last resort, rather than an effective combat tool.

SHOTGUN

DESCRIPTION:

Similar to the Hunting Gun, the Shotgun is deadly over short ranges. However, the five-bullet capacity and tighter scatter make it preferable to the Hunting Gun if you have the choice.

ARMORY NOTES:

The Shotgun rips through Body Armor and cuts down most enemies with a single shell. Get in close for some quick kills.

HARPOON

DESCRIPTION:

Designed for underwater combat, the Harpoon is just as useful on the surface. The only downside is that you must reload after every shot, so it's not a good choice when faced with multiple enemies!

ARMORY NOTES:

The Harpoon is your only underwater weapon. Above the surface, opt for the simple Crossbow and save the Harpoon ammo for combat encounters in the briny deep.

SIMPLE CROSSBOW

DESCRPTION:

With two levels of zoom and a near-silent action, the Crossbow is an ideal weapon when stealth is required. The bow requires a high level of accuracy, so you must aim carefully. Plus, you have to reload after every shot, so make sure you aim for the head to take down your target in one shot.

ARMORY NOTES:

Without a doubt, this is the most fun weapon in your arsenal. Silent and deadly, the simple Crossbow is the only weapon equipped with a scope for long distance kills. Watch for enemies wearing helmets—a single Crossbow bolt will not pierce a helmet. It takes two direct hits from a Crossbow bolt to kill an enemy wearing a helmet.

THREE-ARROWS CROSSBOW

DESCRIPTION:

Similar to the simple Crossbow, this enhanced version holds three arrows, primed simultaneously.

ARMORY NOTES:

Upgrades! This three-shot version of the simple Crossbow keeps you from having to zoom out, reload, and then zoom back in on a group of enemies to score a second kill. Use it when you're faced with multiple targets at a distance.

MINIGUN

DESCRIPTION:

This very powerful hand Submachine Gun is hampered only by its heavy recoil. The magazine holds 32 bullets, but with such a fast fire rate, squeezing the trigger for a couple of seconds will empty it. Like the 9mm, you can hold one in each hand.

ARMORY NOTES:

The rapid rate of fire makes the dual MiniGun a deadly weapon. When you empty both clips into an enemy, he is going down for the count. This one is great for Boss encounters where inflicting maximum damage quickly is a must.

KALASH

DESCRIPTION:

A Russian Submachine Gun, and a favorite among the mercenaries working for the conspiracy.

ARMORY NOTES:

Like the Assault Rifle, the Kalash is less effective over long ranges. It can be fired as a full automatic or in a burst. Switch to burst when you have a limited amount of ammo.

ASSAULT RIFLE

DESCRIPTION:

Similar to the Kalash, the American M16 comes with an additional grenade launcher that, when used well, can be devastating in small areas.

ARMORY NOTES:

The AR Grenade Launcher is indispensable in many combat situations. When an enemy takes cover or you are faced with multiple targets, drop a grenade on their head. Be sure to give yourself enough distance so you don't get caught up in the splash damage.

SMG (SUBMACHINE GUN)

DESCRIPTION:

This is an extremely powerful, heavy Submachine Gun. With the ability to fire off a string of 200 bullets, you should be able to take down even the largest of enemy gatherings. The only flaw is its weight—you'll move slowly when you have the SMG in your hands.

ARMORY NOTES:

Moving slowly makes you an easier target while carrying the SMG. If you have MedKits available, you can use this weapon to clear an entire room of enemies in mere seconds. With 200 rounds, it can dish out a long-lasting supply of death and destruction.

BAZOOKA

DESCRIPTION:

The Bazooka is a truly ferocious weapon capable of taking out vehicles, along with human opponents. You'll need to reload after every shot, but that should just about provide enough time for the smoke to clear. As with the SMG, the Bazooka is a heavy weapon and will prevent you from moving with anything resembling speed.

ARMORY NOTES:

When you're tired of being on the receiving end of Bazooka Rockets, pick up one of these and give a little back! A devastating blast, the Bazooka Rocket can take out three or four enemies at once, and is great over long ranges.

SNIPER RIFLE

DESCRIPTION:

The Sniper Rifle provides deadly accuracy at long range, and has a shot as powerful as any Assault Rifle. With a 10-bullet magazine and two levels of zoom, it's the perfect tool for eliminating far away, stubborn enemies.

ARMORY NOTES:

Head shot! Head shot! Head shot! With the Sniper Rifle in your hands, enemies are like ducks in a barrel. Find a nice, safe hiding spot and eliminate them from long distance.

GRENADE

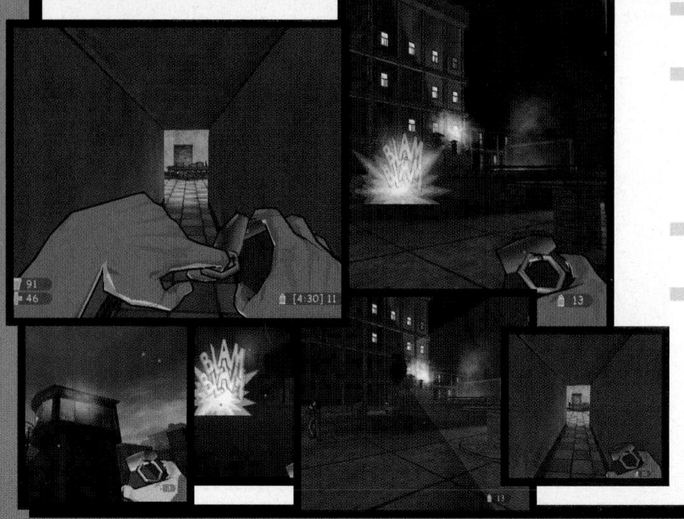

DESCRIPTION:

When you pull the pin, a fuse timer inside the Grenade starts ticking. Smart enemies will try to flee when they see a Grenade coming, so be sure to judge the timing of your throw so they're unable to get out of the way.

ARMORY NOTES:

A Grenade can be as big of a hazard to you as it is to the enemy. Watch your throw so that they don't bounce back in your face, and avoid using Grenades in close-quarters combat or you'll get caught up in the splash damage. Burn away enough of the timer so that your enemy doesn't have time to run and hide.

OBJECTS

MEDKIT

This enables you to pick up 25 or 50 health points (if you have acquired the "medical care" skill).

FULL MEDKIT

Pick up 50 or 100 health points with one of these (if you have acquired the "medical care" skill).

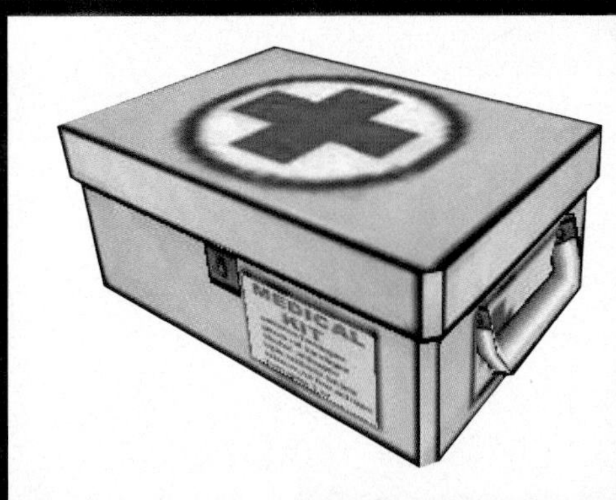

KEY

Each key corresponds to a particular door. You'll find many of keys on the guards.

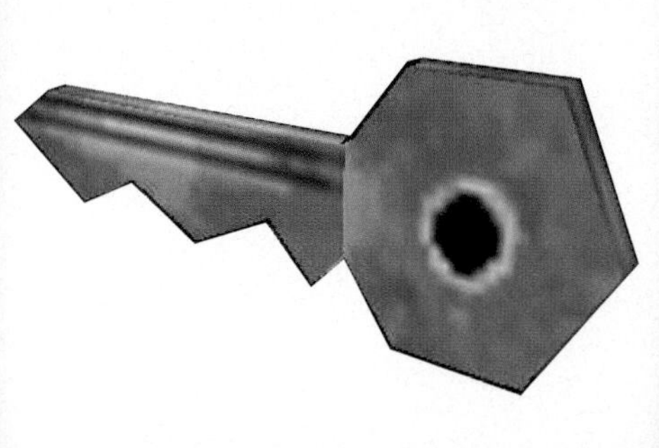

LOCKPICK

This is an essential tool for picking even the most stubborn locks.

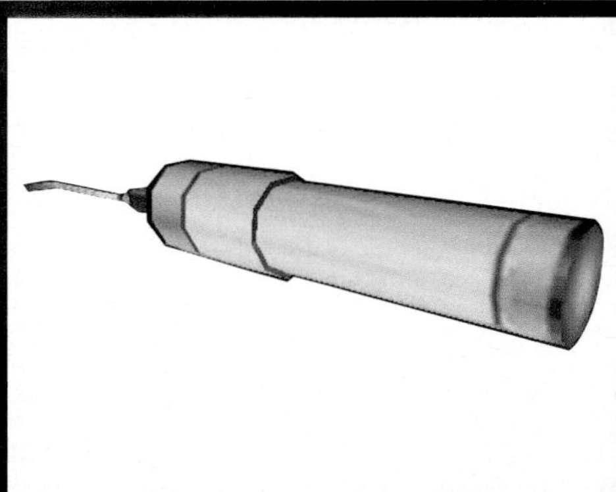

MAGNETIC PASS

The best-protected buildings use this highly sophisticated security system.

GRAPPLING HOOK

Both indoors and out, this tool will help you access the most hard-to-reach corners of the game.

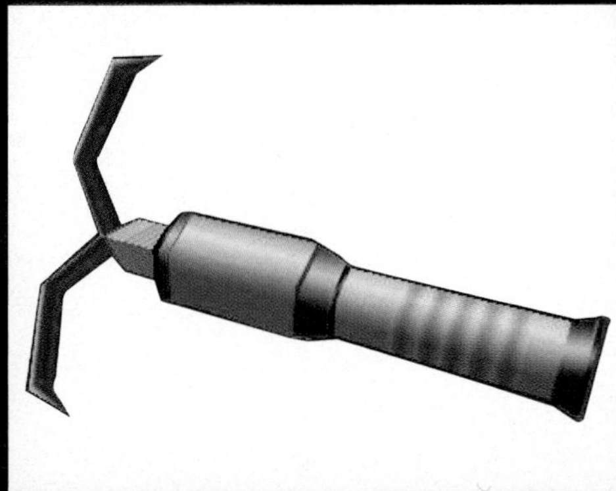

Do you think you can make it to the truck?
50
68
HOOK
48
WINSLOW
100
In your deposition you even added... that you don't feel like
FBI
100

Ohhh... Thank you, thank you!

Mission 1:
ON THE BEACH

Place the reticule on the helicopter to trigger a dream sequence.

CHECKPOINT: REACH THE TRUCK

This is the shortest and potentially most frustrating mission in the game. If you don't trigger the dream sequence, the mission is unending.

Follow the lifeguard up the beach and wait for her verbal queue of "Huh...?" Focus your reticule on the helicopter coming over the dune to trigger a dream sequence.

Follow the lifeguard up the beach until you pass out to end the mission.

Mission 2:
FIRST-AID POST

QUICK AND DIRTY

Get into the back room, grab the **Key**, and wipe out the enemy at the back door. Return to the front room, pop the thug, and use the key on the front door.

Eliminate the two enemies coming from the pier and take the weapons off the corpses. Head up the pier and pick off the sniper from the top of the cliff.

Run up the pier and shoot the enemy hidden behind the cliff face to the left, then continue down the pier, pop the knife-throwing thug, and get down to the marina.

There are a few thugs near the exit, but no major challenges. Hug the right cliff face, then shoot the enemy in the back-right area of the clearing and steal his **Key**.

Walk up to the truck, use the Key, and open the door.

MISSION BRIEFING

OBJECTIVES

Escape from the first-aid post. Leave the beach using the killer's pick-up truck.

WEAPONS

Throwing Knife	44 Special
9mm	Kalash

ENEMIES

Helicopter
Various Thugs

SUMMARY

After passing out and waking in the first-aid post, get ready for your first taste of action. This is a short introductory mission that pits you against a bunch of thugs. However, use this mission to get a feel for the game and the few weapons you're given.

CHECKPOINT:
ESCAPE FROM THE FIRST-AID POST

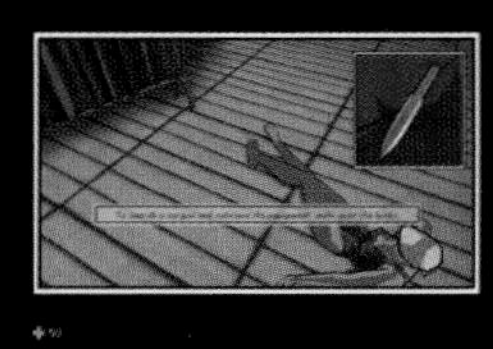

Grab the **Throwing Knives** from the dead lifeguard's body and slip into the back room. Close the door (use the action button), then grab the **9mm** and the **9mm Ammo** from the table on the right. Turn to the left and grab the **Key** off the next table.

MISSION TRAINING

Everything you need is called out in this first mission. Every weapon, piece of ammo, and MedKit is detailed in the walkthrough. Use this mission to learn what to loot from the enemies (and when) during future missions.

However, in later missions, we only cover items or weapons found off the beaten track. In addition, the first appearance of any weapon on a particular level is identified, but not every occurrence.

Look out! The enemy has covered the back door, as well. Slip into the corner and take out the henchmen with a few shots (or just one well-chosen ping to the head).

Exit the back door, grab the thug's **44 Special**, and the **Box of 44 Ammo** from the bench. Instead of returning to the first-aid post, continue around the deck to the other side.

Equip the 44 Special, then turn back to the post and look through the front window. You should see the enemy at the front door milling about. Take a few pot shots through the window to eliminate him without endangering yourself.

BRING DOWN THE CHOPPER

Don't waste a single bullet on the enemies. Grab all the 44 Special Ammo, then go to the only end of the deck where the helicopter is visible.

Empty the 44 Special on the helicopter until you're out of ammo, then switch to the 9mm and do the same.

Finally, to finish it off, take the Kalash off the dead thug, and walk up the pier to the set of four crates in the center. Fire on the helicopter until it's toast!

You won't have much ammo after this battle, but there is enough to finish the mission.

Walk back through the first-aid post and into the front room. Take the **MedKit** from the cabinet and use the Key on the front door. Slip out onto the dock, grab the **Kalash**, and duck back into the post.

PLACE THE BAIT

If you need to prompt the helicopter and enemies to leave their spot on the end of the pier, get out onto the dock, look to the right, and force their hand by getting off a few shots from your 9mm.

Head out onto the pier, take the **9mm Ammo** from the corpses, and take the **5.56 Ammo** off of the crate. Instead of facing the rest of the enemies immediately, turn to the right and run along the row of shops. Get the **Full MedKit** from the first-aid cabinet on the last shop.

Head back to the main path and take a right. Watch out! There's a henchman roaming the cliff top. Pick him off from afar using the 44 Special, then run up and grab the ammo off of his body. A thug ambushes you from the left, but it's nothing you can't handle. A few quick shots remove this threat. Take his **9mm Ammo** and continue on.

Again, there's an enemy perched on the cliff top to the right. Use your trusty 44 Special to peg him from long range. A knife-throwing henchman tries to ambush you as you run up the pier. Introduce him to the pain of the

STEALTH RUN

There's an alternative tactic to facing all of the enemies in the marina. As soon as you can, jump into the water and submerge. Swim along and hug the cliff to your right. Keep an eye on your oxygen gauge; if it gets too low, take a breath and go back under again. You'll only miss out on a MedKit and some ammo—not that much.

Don't bother wasting any shots at the boat. Follow the pier around the bend and take the second dock on the left. Pick off the enemy waiting at the end, take the **44 Ammo** off his corpse, and then hop into the yellow boat on the left for another **MedKit.**

As you approach the end of the pier, an enemy could be waiting on the right. However, if he's not in the bushes, look for him near the truck. Wherever he dies, make sure to nab the **44 Ammo** from his body. Hug the cliff face to the right, sneak behind the kiosk, and grab the **MedKit** from the cabinet, as well as the **Box of 44 Ammo** on the crate.

Shoot the enemy in the head and loot his body for the **Key**, then run up to the driver's side of the truck and unlock the door to end the mission. Well done, XIII!

MISSION COMPLETE

Mission 3:
WINSLOW BANK

MISSION BRIEFING

OBJECTIVES

Access the strongroom. Do not kill the bank staff.

WEAPONS

9mm
44 Special
Shotgun

ENEMIES

Bank Guard (innocent)
Various Thugs

SUMMARY

The Winslow Bank holds a key to your forgotten past, XIII. It's time to discover another piece to the puzzle that is your life. Be ready, though, because things won't end as one would think.

QUICK AND DIRTY

Give the Winslow Bank key to the clerk, then follow him to the strongroom. Enter the vault and open your safe to trigger the dream sequence.

Move through the bank, knocking the guards unconscious, and get to the director's office.

Grab the Magnetic Card off the desk, then use it to access the elevator on the balcony.

Continue your escape by climbing down the fire escape to complete the mission.

CHECKPOINT: ENTER THE BANK

Walk toward the second counter on the left and address the clerk. He recognizes you as Mr. Rowland—interesting. You'll hand him the Winslow Bank Key you received from the lifeguard before she was killed. Walk to the guard on your left and wait for the clerk to open the door.

Follow the clerk to the second security door, then down toward the antechamber to the vault. Your objective is behind the monstrous door. Head to the back of the vault to find your safe.

DON'T BE RUDE

If you try to get to the other bank teller, the bank patron tells you to wait in line like everyone else. Take her advice, she'll be a while.

Open the safe and remove the laptop to trigger another dream sequence. Get behind the enigmatic woman and listen to her conversation as you follow her back to the safe. When she tells you to arm the bomb, place the reticule on it.

SAFETY FIRST

As soon as you grab the laptop, slip to the right and get away from the safe.

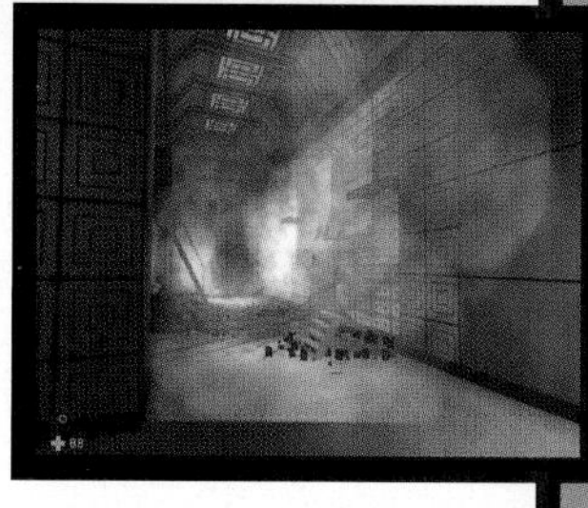

When the dream sequence ends, you should return to your current body, well away from the safe. If you didn't run away, do so now or else you'll take heavy damage from the explosion that's about to occur.

The bomb blows a hole in the wall; that's your escape route, XIII! Ignore the bank clerk's inquiries and run through the opening. Continue along the shaft and up the ladder. Crouch to enter the ventilation shaft, then follow it to the end and punch the grate to reach the next checkpoint.

CHECKPOINT: ESCAPE THE BANK

Quickly eliminate the guard at the end of the hall by sneaking up and hitting him from behind. Take too long and he'll turn around and start firing. In this case, take him out with punches, then grab the **44 Special**.

As the police scanners start referring to gunshots at Winslow Bank, continue your escape and head up the stairs. Take the chair and prepare to bludgeon the next guard since it won't be easy to sneak up on him.

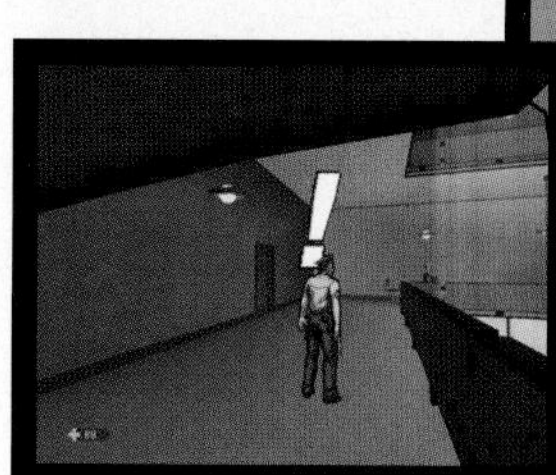

Head around the balcony and grab another chair. There's a single guard on the longer sides of the balcony, so be careful. Duck behind the partitions and wait for the guards to get close enough before whacking them with the chairs. The chairs break whether you hit the guards or not. If you miss, use your best brawling skills to finish the job. Make sure to take the **44 Ammo** from their comatose bodies.

Open the last door on the left, then quickly grab a chair and hide in the corner next to the closed door. Another guard patrols this area, so prepare to waste him. There's a **MedKit** on the far shelf; grab it and move into the director's office.

There's nothing to take in this area, but check out the symbol marked on the case of cash. The next room has two patrolling guards that aren't as easy to get rid of. Use chairs whenever possible and resort to your fists when you must. When they're down and relieved of ammo, grab the **MedKit** and jump onto the table. Crouch down, smash the grate, and move into the adjacent hallway.

CHECKPOINT: THE ESCAPE CONTINUES

You're prompted to take a hostage and, luckily, there's one waiting in the room at the end of the hall. Sneak up, grab her, and take the **Magnetic Card** from the table. Use it to bypass the security keypad next to the door, then unlock it. Keeping the hostage between you and the three guards outside the door, head out and then back up to the right.

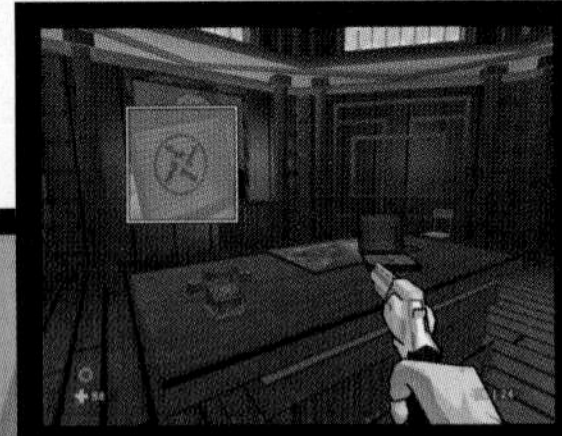

HOSTAGES

Taking hostages is a key element to gameplay. Use the Action Button when sneaking up behind an opponent instead of the Fire Button, and utitlize hostages as human shields.

Note, however, that only live hostages work. Picking up a dead body (or an unconscious one) won't protect you from your enemies.

Back up around the corner and hug the wall to the left, then make your way to the elevator. Press really close to the wall and try to keep the hostage between you and the guards. If they get a shot, your traveling companion will take it. Back into the elevator, press the down button, and then knock your hostage out.

Get ready, XIII—this is when the escape turns deadly. Some goons have infiltrated the bank to take you out, and they're not worried about offing a few bank guards in the process. Dodge to the right, take the **44 Ammo** off the guard's corpse, then walk toward the rail. Shoot the thug across the balcony. (It's easier to pick him off from long range than face-to-face.)

Reload the 44 Special and dash into the door straight ahead. Pop the thug on the left and take his ammo, then grab the **Shotgun** from the dead guard's corpse and move to the left of the next door. There's another hoodlum just waiting to show you how tough he is—dash his illusions. Return to the balcony, grab any ammo, and move toward the open door to the left as you exit. Another thug's on the way.

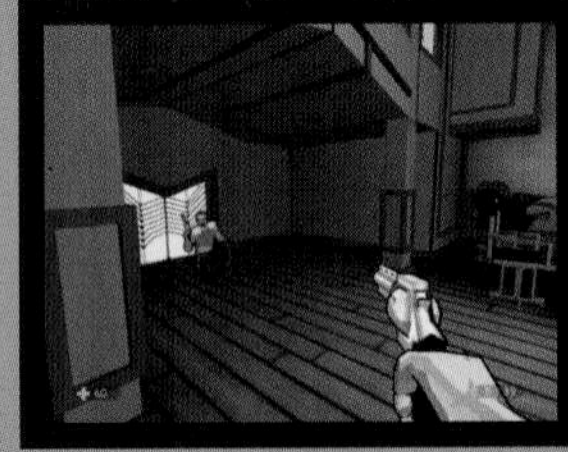

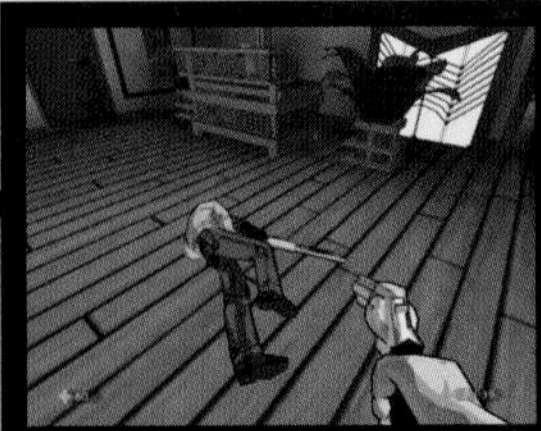

Grab your latest victim's **9mm** and enter the door from which this attacker emerged. Enter the doorway with the blinking light to the right. Look up as you walk out and pick off the final thug in the area.

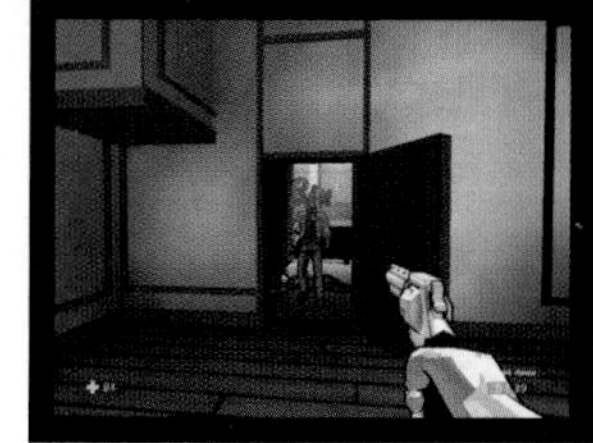

Climb down the fire escape and carefully descend the ladder. Once you reach the bottom, holster your weapon. Although you're on the business end of a bunch of weapons, these agents won't take you out... yet.

A mysterious, one-armed stranger takes you into FBI custody. The pieces of the puzzle are starting to fall into place.

MISSION COMPLETE

Mission 4: UNDER ARREST: BROOKLYN

MISSION BRIEFING

OBJECTIVES

Neutralize the FBI agents. Escape FBI Headquarters.
Rendezvous with the woman on the roof.

WEAPONS

9mm	Shotgun
44 Special	Frag Grenade

ENEMIES

FBI Agents (innocents)
Various Thugs

SUMMARY

XIII, you've been captured and are being held in the FBI Headquarters in Brooklyn. Get out of there, but don't kill any agents. Use your stealth skills to avoid contact with the G-men, and weapon efficiency to remove the threat imposed by those hunting you.

QUICK AND DIRTY

No Keys or Magnetic Cards are in this mission, it's just a straightforward escape plan. Move through the ventilation shafts and halls of the FBI HQ and refrain from killing any agents.

The brutes that block your path are another matter entirely—shoot on sight. Reach the hole in the brick wall and the ladder beyond to end the mission.

CHECKPOINT: ESCAPE FBI HEADQUARTERS

A great deal of information is exchanged during the beginning of this mission. Steve Rowland is recorded to have been dead for two years and you were seen assassinating the President of the United States. The enigmatic woman reappears and drops the name "Mongoose." Who's that?

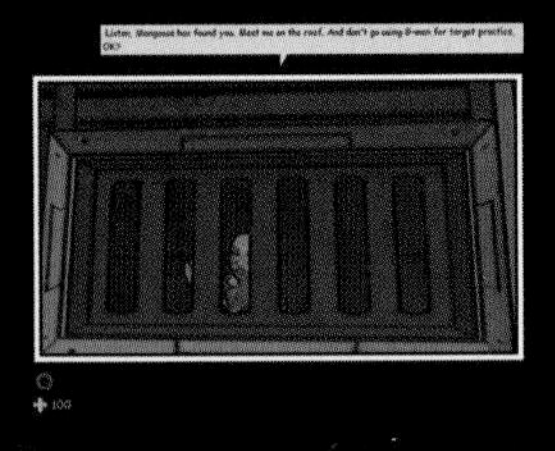

Once free of your handcuffs, walk over to the woman and learn more about your new objectives. It seems you're destined to rendezvous with her on the roof, XIII.

There's nothing in the cabinets along the wall, so get through the door and head to the right—away from the voices. Crouch down, punch the grate, and use the ventilation shaft as an escape route. Smash the grate at the end of the shaft and quickly grab the chair by the door. Smash it over the guard's head as he enters, being careful not to hit the door with the chair in the process.

The cabinets in this room are full of goodies. There's a **Full MedKit** in the cabinet on the right and a **MedKit** and a **Box of 9mm Ammo** in the center cabinet. There are also some bottles in the center cabinet if you want to smash them over the heads of some FBI guards. Grab the **9mm** off the guard on the floor and get ready to head out.

Take the chair across the hall and turn right. There's an unarmed guard asking you not to hurt him, but a bump on the head is better than a bullet in the gut. Smack him and grab one of the chairs flanking the door, because there's another guard in the room and he's armed. Break the chair over his head, then smash the cartons in front of the vent.

Enter the shaft. As you do, guards throughout the hallways are exclaiming that someone's storming the building. Yes, XIII, your old friends are back to remove you from the equation, but why?

Slip across the hallway and into the ventilation shaft on the opposite wall.

GOOD SAMARITAN

Look down the hallway to the right as you enter the shaft. There's a thug in a gray coat trying to off some agents, but you can stop him. If you don't, the next segment of the mission is easier, but there's something to say about doing the right thing.

Make it to the end of the shaft and grab the chair in the hallway. Knock out the agent, then punch the lights out of the one that comes to his aid. Grab the **44 Special** and the **Frag Grenade** from their bodies. That Frag Grenade is definitely a nice thing to have.

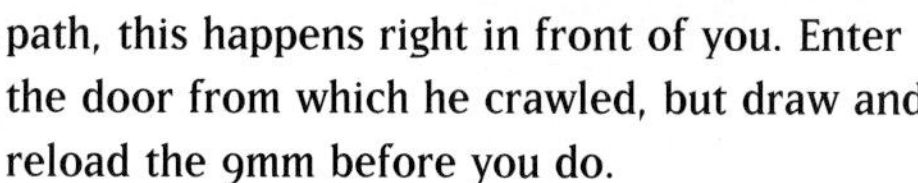

Turn back and head toward the end of the hallway. The inset window shows a G-man crawling out of a door; if you chose the correct path, this happens right in front of you. Enter the door from which he crawled, but draw and reload the 9mm before you do.

Strafe past the door while looking in to draw the hoodlum's attention. Wait for him to get a few shots off and reload before going for the doorway and shooting him in the head. Shoot the other thug as he enters. Grab the **44 Ammo** and equip the 44 Special. As you exit the room, you notice an agent being chased by another goon. Be careful not to hit the agent and pop the goon in the noggin.

Run down the hall and enter the office on the left. There's a **MedKit** in the left cabinet, and a thug threatening an agent in the office just beyond. Try to peg him before he gets a shot off, then take his **Shotgun** and the **12 Ammo** from the cabinet.

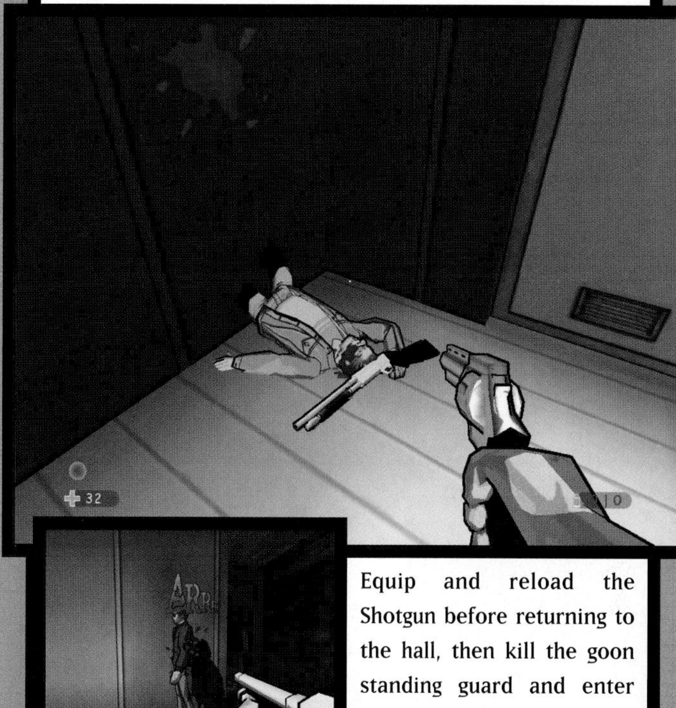

Equip and reload the Shotgun before returning to the hall, then kill the goon standing guard and enter the hole in the wall to exit the FBI headquarters.

CHECKPOINT: GET TO THE ROOF

Open the doors at the top of the stairs while equipping and reloading the 44 Special. Unfortunately, you shouldn't have too many bullets left, but it's stronger than the 9mm. Run to the wall ahead, then slip down and open both doors. Back up to wait for the two goons to enter, then give them the appropriately violent welcome.

Reload your gun, run toward the wall with the door, and enter the doorway. Repeat the tactic used last time to kill the three enemies set on murdering you. One of them has more **44 Ammo**. Run to the back-left corner of the next room and descend the stairs. Take the **Shotgun, 12 Ammo,** and **MedKit** in the cabinet.

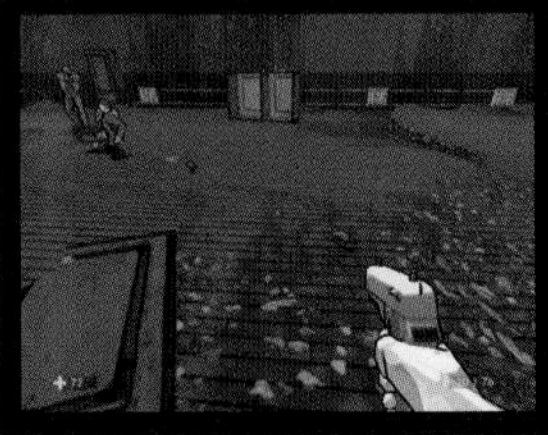

FRAG 'EM

The next room presents a perfect opportunity to use the Frag Grenade you collect from the knocked out agent. Toss it toward the back-left corner of the room and back up.

There's a large section of the floor missing in the next room. Take out the two goons on the bottom level, and then the two that appear across the chasm. Two rooms away, there's a ramp leading to the bottom level. Follow it down (to avoid the falling damage). There's a **Heavy Vest** in the back corner of the room on the first floor.

QUICK DROP

If you want to drop to the next level, land on the two adjacent cabinets, then jump off.

Loot the corpses and head back up the ramp. Run directly into the room ahead and kill the Shotgun-armed thugs in the room to the right (three in all). Follow the rooms to a new hallway behind the walls. It leads to a hole in the wall and a ladder to the exit.

MISSION COMPLETE

Mission 5:
ON THE ROOFTOPS

MISSION BRIEFING

OBJECTIVES

Follow Major Jones to the exit.
Protect Jones.

WEAPONS

9mm
44 Special
Frag Grenade
Grenade
Shotgun
Sniper Rifle
RPG Rocket
Launcher

ENEMIES

Various Thugs
Snipers
RPG Launcher

SUMMARY

XIII, Major Jones is under your protection on this mission. There are a few firefights ahead, so keep an eye on her, as well as your ammo supply. You'll also learn to use the Hook. This is a very intense mission, so keep a cool head and get ready for some heat!

QUICK AND DIRTY

Follow Major Jones and use your Hook to ascend to the rooftop. Take the Sniper Rifle from Jones and pick off a couple of snipers.

Continue following Jones and search each building for extra ammo and MedKits.

Take out all the thugs between you and Jones' path. There are a bunch.

Destroy the security system preventing access to the helipad.

When the coast is clear, join Jones in the chopper to complete your escape.

CHECKPOINT: MAJOR JONES

Run straight ahead and climb the ladder to rendezvous with Major Jones. She fills you in on the status and gets moving. She also gives you a Hook and demonstrates its use. Aim the Hook at the target above. Swing back and forth while... well, dangling on the Hook, and aim for the rooftop ahead.

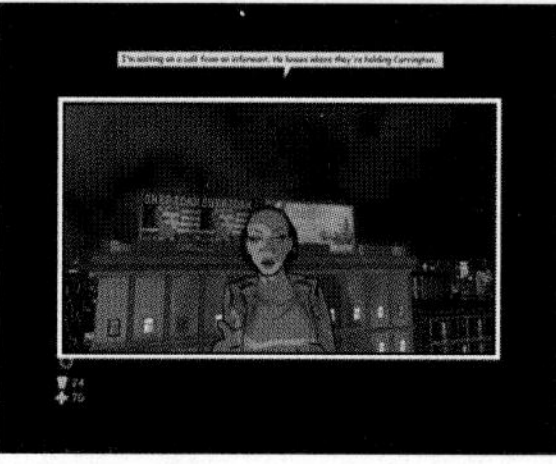

Look at the target rooftop, swing back and forth, and descend while above the roof. Press the Action Button to release the Hook, and then equip another weapon. Walk over to Jones to hear more of what she has to say.

Carrington: Another name that stirs a memory. However, there's no time to dwell on it since your enemies have found you! Follow Jones behind cover, and take the weapon she offers—a **Sniper Rifle**. There are only two targets to snipe.

1. The first can be shot from behind your current cover. Move to the left side and switch to your scope (x3). Find the sniper in front of the "N" in the billboard stating "President." Make the shot count by shooting him in the head.

2. Place your right arm against the left side of the structure that you're using for cover, and move ahead. The second sniper is shooting from the building to the right. Again, a headshot conserves ammo.

There are enemies down below, and Jones has offered to cover your descent. Equip the Hook and descend to the rooftop below. Take cover behind the structure ahead and wipe out the enemies waiting for you to arrive.

HIT THE ROOF

Don't try to land on the structure ahead. If you jump off of it to the rooftop, you'll die.

HOOKED SNIPING

It's possible to equip a weapon once you're hooked. It's an interesting challenge to pick off the two enemies firing on you while you're swinging in the air. Although you are certainly more of a target than a threat in this situation, it's still possible to defeat the opposition.

It's time to use some tactical expertise, XIII. Wait behind the structure and lure the enemies into a position that's on your terms. Equip the Shotgun and get ready to blow some holes in the thugs. Take the two out that approach from the right and loot their corpses; there's some ammo and a **MedKit.** Slip to the left instead of entering the fray.

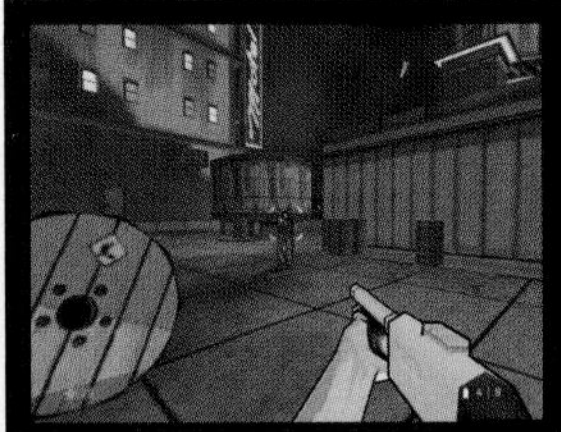

Sneak behind the building ahead, take the **Grenade** from the body on the ground, and then switch to the Sniper Rifle. Target the thug guarding the door ahead and fire! This prompts Jones to improve her position. Equip the Shotgun once again and move forward to cover her. Two goons emerge from the building and appear on your right. Drop them!

There's **12 Ammo** and a **MedKit** in the building. As you pass, Jones makes it to the door and unlocks it. From inside, you hear another enemy preparing for your approach. Reload, get through the door, and aim to the left of the flipped table. Take the **MedKit** from behind the table and move to the other door.

Follow Jones up the fire escape and get ready to use a new skill. There's a gap in the path ahead so you'll need to get a running start to make the jump. However, pause at the second landing to listen to the news report.

CHECKPOINT: CLEAR THE ROOFTOPS

Don't jump until you're at the very end of the highest landing. If you jump before that point, XIII will fall to his death.

Open the door. Two goons flee from sight—one to the left and the other to the right. The one on the left is crouched in the corner, so aim low. The other attacks when his partner goes down. A Shotgun blast to the face is enough for him. A **Light Vest** is among the ammo on their bodies.

BM650 Ammo is on the shelf, two **Sniper Rifles** are flanking the cabinet, and a **Full MedKit** is on the floor to the left. Once you've cleared the room of everything useful, equip and reload the Sniper Rifle.

RELOAD

This is a good time to do a full reload on all your weapons. Always consider doing this after completing a section that required a lot of ammo.

Move to the left corner of the skylight and look directly across it. There are three snipers firing from the rooftop—one on left side and two on the front. Shoot each of them while drawing fire from Major Jones.

Follow Major Jones and leap across the chasm between the buildings to land on a stack of crates. Trail her to the gate and cover her as you both storm the rooftop. Reload the Shotgun and wait for the major to do her thing.

Five thugs immediately appear. One of them runs screaming across the rooftop and through a window across the way. Two emerge from the building on the left, and another pair is near the building that the major blew up. Eliminate the foes closest to Jones first; protecting her is still one of your primary objectives.

Now turn your attention to the two thugs near the other building. There's a **Full MedKit** in the building that's still standing. Don't miss it, XIII. Follow Jones across the other gap, through the hall, and into another room.

CHECKPOINT: GET TO THE CHOPPER

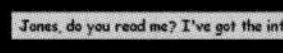

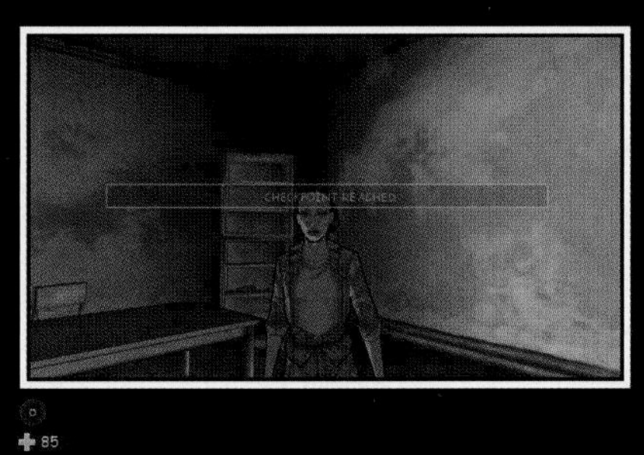

Listen in on the message from Jones' contact, but be ready for action. Quickly switch to the Sniper Rifle and move behind the major. Snipe the first enemy to the right, and then look to the left. There should be a gap between the doorframe and the wall. Use the gap to maintain cover, and target the most dangerous enemy out there: the guy with the RPG.

Quickly exit the room and target the goon to the left of the stairs across the rooftop. When he's out of commission, a replacement runs in front of your scope. Pop him and switch to the Shotgun as you run ahead. Take out the final enemy and get ready to disable the security system.

ROCKET GOODNESS

Grab the Rocket Launcher from the thug's body and feel free to use it at will. However, don't let Major Jones get near the blast.

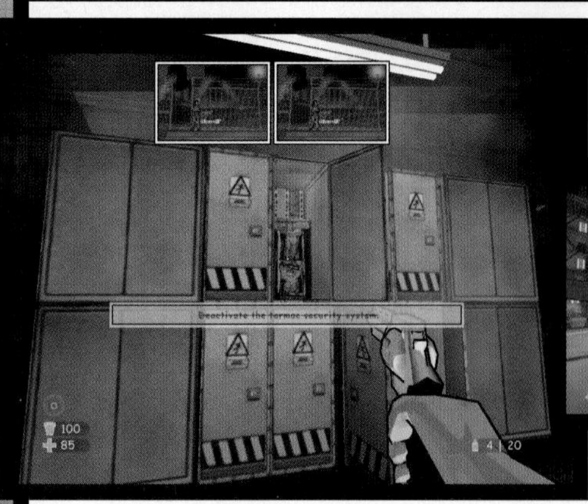

Enter the building on the right and use your special disarming tool to finish the job. That is to say, shoot the system with your Shotgun.

Follow Major Jones onto the helipad and head immediately to the right. Two enemies emerge from the building in the back corner, and one of them is armed with Grenades—he's wearing a green jacket and glasses. When the last two thugs in the level fall to your onslaught, approach the chopper and get out of there!

PREVENTIVE MEDICINE

Try firing a rocket at the back corner as you reach the helipad. You might just slay both enemies with a single shot. Of course, if you miss, fire another.

MISSION COMPLETE

Mission 6: ENTER MILITARY BASE HUALPAR

QUICK AND DIRTY

Work through the patrols to the first bunker.

Restore power to the extendable bridge by using the switch in the bunker.

Wipe out the soldiers along the path, extend the bridge, and make your way across.

Ascend to the mountain ledge and enter the exterior ventilation shaft.

MISSION BRIEFING

OBJECTIVE

Enter the military base.

WEAPONS

9mm
Shotgun
Crossbow
Assault Rifle

ENEMIES

Soldiers

SUMMARY

Prepare yourself, XIII. You're equipped with some new weapons, but they'll soon feel like old friends in your experienced hands. Work your way through the enemy patrols and maintain your covert presence throughout the mission.

CHECKPOINT: QUIET ENTRY

Equip the Shotgun and move down the path. When you notice the enemy soldier over body of a downed guard, get up there and shoot him before he shoots you, then equip the Crossbow.

Walk, don't run, up to the end of the path. When you're close, switch to sniper mode (3x). There are three soldiers to the left; use a single bolt on each. The safest shot for the first two is between the road marker and the mountainside. To kill the next, move out into the clearing a little bit.

Remove the weapons and ammo from the bodies. The only item new to you is the **Assault Rifle**. There are also two **MedKits** in the guard house. While you're looting, two more soldiers approach from the direction where you need to go. The Shotgun works best at close range and the Crossbow is ideal from the confines of the guardhouse.

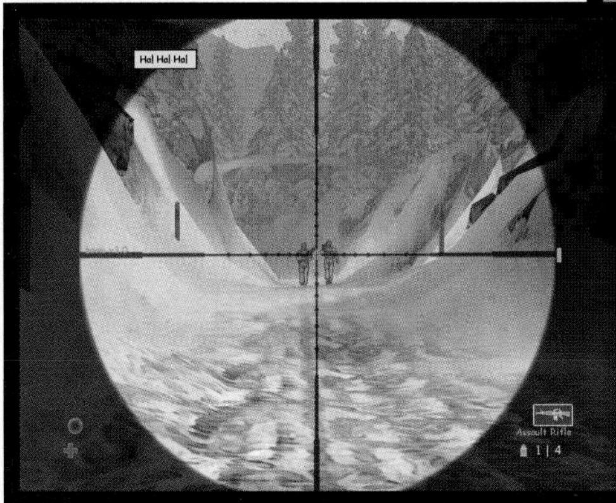

Walk up the road while keeping to the right. Switch to the Crossbow's sniper mode when the whole truck is visible. Two enemy soldiers are on the left side. Shoot them quickly or else one may get away. Move up the path and switch to your sniper mode (x8) when you see movement up ahead.

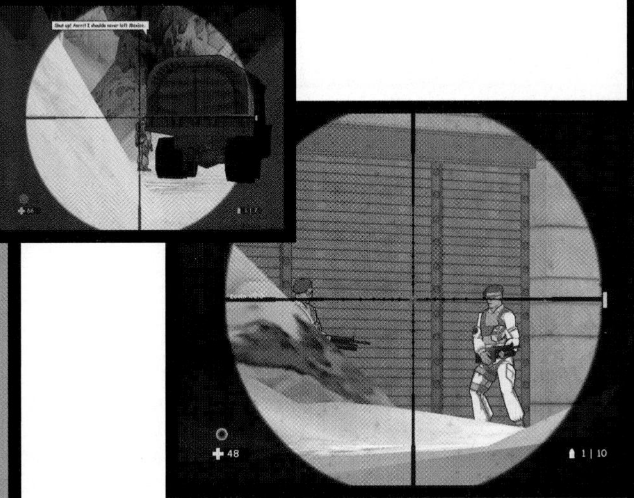

Securing the bunker on the left is your next objective. Enter with the Shotgun drawn. It seems that the enemy soldiers are still clearing it out. Fire at the two soldiers and clean up the mess. A **Heavy Vest** and a **Light Helmet** are on the crates near the entrance.

Quickly move to the back-right corner of the room; walk backwards to cover yourself. Three enemy soldiers storm the bunker while you're still inside; it seems that your activities have been discovered. Wipe them out and snag the **Full MedKit, M16 Grenades,** and **Box of M16 Ammo** from the barrels in the back.

Climb to the second level and immediately restore power to the bridge. Walk along the balcony to the left, and then grab everything off the back corner (**M16 Grenades,** a **MedKit**, and **Ammo**). Take cover behind the crates and use the Crossbow to snipe any soldiers that try to re-establish their presence in the bunker.

HELMETS PREVENT INJURY

It takes two perfect headshots to kill a soldier wearing a helmet. The first one destroys the helmet and the second punctures the skull.

Jump onto the truck, then down to the floor. With the bunker cleared of enemies and power restored to the bridge, move on to the bridge itself. Grab your Crossbow and get ready for some more sniping fun.

Run to the left and take cover behind the guardhouse. Peek to the left side of the guard room and look up the mountainside. There's a soldier armed with a Crossbow atop the ridge. When he's down, check out the grate on the ledge he's protecting—remember it.

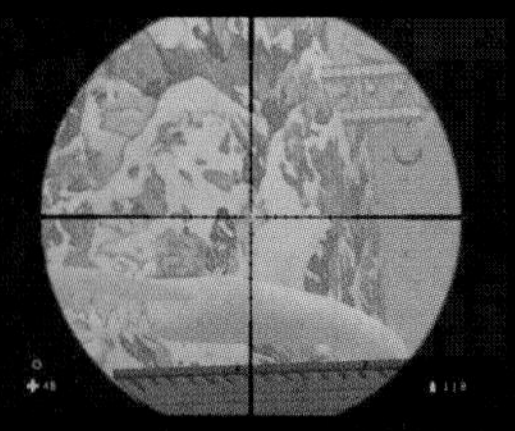

Arm yourself with the Shotgun, enter the guardhouse, and take out the lone soldier stationed there. Approach the controls and use them to extend the bridge. Move to the right of the guardhouse and use it for cover once more. There's a sniper patrolling the wall at the end of the ravine.

Run across the bridge and approach the building on the left. There are soldiers inside, but you need not face them directly. Look at them through the window, fire a bullet at the glass, and then quickly lob an M16 Grenade through the opening. Before entering and looting the bodies, run to the guardhouse on this side of the bridge and retract it. This prevents any soldiers from approaching from the other side.

Get back into the building with the dead soldiers and grab whatever you can off their bodies. There's a **Full MedKit** and some **Bolts** on the shelves to the right. Don't miss the **Shotgun** on top of the crates.

Use the crates on the left of the barracks to reach the roof. Hook onto the target above and pull yourself up to the mountain ledge. Nab the Bolts off the soldier and move to the grate.

CLIMB THE MOUNTAIN

Run up the mountainside near the crates and jump onto the highest one. This way, you don't need to complete a tough series of jumps.

Waste two bolts on the soldiers across the bridge if you want, but the main objective is to enter the base. Break the grate and move toward the end of the shaft, then drop into the room and climb down the ladder.

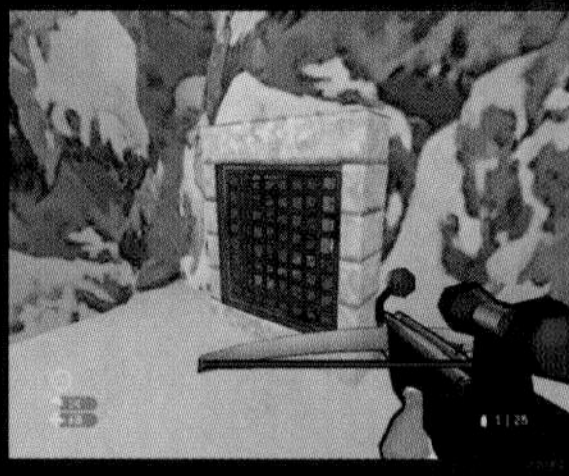

MISSION COMPLETE

Mission 7:

INFILTRATE MILITARY BASE HUALPAR

MISSION BRIEFING

OBJECTIVES

Avoid the SPADS and disarm the alarm.
Infiltrate the base.

WEAPONS

9mm
Crossbow
Shotgun
Assault Rifle

ENEMIES

Soldiers

SUMMARY

This mission is all about stealth, XIII. Your Crossbow and Throwing Knives should be your main weapons. Covertly take down any patrolling guards and shoot from the shadows. Disable the alarm by destroying the four Generators.

QUICK AND DIRTY

Destroy the four Generators (two outside the enclosed area and two within).

Climb to the top of the wall.

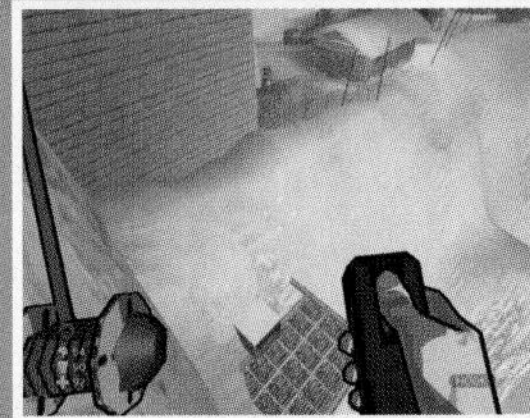

Descend into the grate that leads to the base.

CHECKPOINT: ENTERING THE BASE

Break through the grate and drop to the cover behind the crates. Take the **Crossbow** and **Bolts** from behind the crates and slowly move out. Cross to the other stack of crates and take the **Throwing Knives** from atop them.

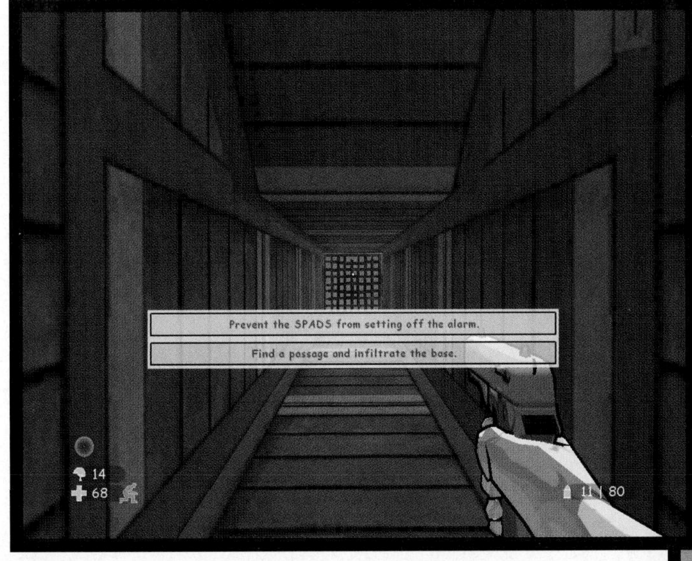

Move to the left section of the area and sneak up to the third barrier. Hide behind it and wait to hear the soldier's footsteps fade, then move to the opening and aim in the direction where you heard the sound. Look through the gap between the barrier and target the blinking red light—a soldier appears soon enough. Take him down with your Crossbow.

Make your way to the soldier's body and take the **Throwing Knives** on the nearby crates. Move to the far-left end of the bunker. Glance into the window to check out the soldiers inside. Another M16 Grenade works well here. Not only do you kill the two guards inside, but you also disable one of the four **Generators**.

Walk around the right side of the bunker and pick the corpses clean. There are also some **Throwing Knives** and a **MedKit** on the desks inside. Walk out to the left and hide behind the crates. Continue slowly moving up, using the crates for cover, and snipe the soldier patrolling the area outside the next bunker.

LOCKPICK

This is the first time that you need to use your Lockpick. Each lock you pick takes a certain amount of time—the harder the lock, the longer the time required to pick it. Keep this in mind and eliminate any patrolling enemies. Getting shot in the back while you're working on a lock is as embarrassing as it is painful.

The next bunker is unlocked. Enter and check the cabinets for the **Light Helmet**, **Throwing Knives,** and the **MedKit** within.

Slip out the door and up to the next guardhouse. There's a Shotgun inside and another **Generator** to destroy.

Continue along the wall and walk up to the bunker protruding from it. Use it as cover and aim your Crossbow (x3) at the door and crates ahead. Wait for it to steady, then take down the soldier patrolling the area.

Cross to the tanker and head for the door leading to the closed-off area. Draw the Crossbow and pick the lock. There should be a soldier patrolling straight ahead. Put a bolt in his head, then move through the doorway and turn right. There's a guard or two patrolling behind the first barracks. You know what to do, XIII.

Slip along the wall to the right and dispatch the guard near the tank. Make it to the back corner and the building with the blinking red light mounted next to the door. The voices from within give the soldiers away. Pick the lock, equip your M16, then open the door and toss an M16 Grenade into the room. Both soldiers and the **Generator** succumb to the blast.

There's a **Light Helmet** on one desk and **Throwing Knives** on another. Exit, move to the right wall, and take out the final patrolling guard in this enclosed area. The guardhouse straight ahead holds the final **Generator**.

There aren't any more soldiers in the area, and the four Generators have been destroyed. Clean out the only two barracks that are unlocked. A **Crossbow, Throwing Knives, Bolts,** a **Shotgun**, and a **MedKit** are stored inside. Exit the door where you entered, then move to the tanker truck and toward the entrance to the barracks on the right.

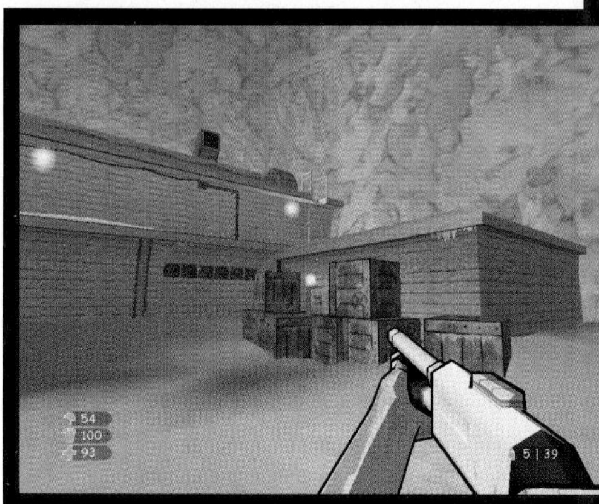

Pick the lock on the door and draw your Shotgun. Wait until the soldier's footsteps are right in front of the door before rushing in and shooting him in the head. Turn to the right and use the same technique to take down the soldier in the barracks. Check the cabinets for a **MedKit** and some **Throwing Knives.**

Exit the barracks and climb the ladder straight ahead. Crouch behind the crates when you reach the top, then draw your Crossbow and peek around the edge. Target the soldier and fire.

Proceed to the end of the path and use the Hook to lower yourself down to the ledge. There's a grate to enter. Make your way through the shaft and break the grate at the other end to finish the mission.

MISSION COMPLETE

Mission 8:
SET GENERAL CARRINGTON FREE

MISSION BRIEFING

OBJECTIVES

Locate General Carrington's cell and release him.

WEAPONS

9mm	Assault Rifle
Crossbow	AR Grenades
Shotgun	Grenades

ENEMIES

Soldiers

SUMMARY

You made it inside the base, XIII. Now you must find General Carrington and free him. He may hold the key to your identity. Stealth is optional.

CHECKPOINT: EAVESDROP ON THE CONVERSATION

After you enter the base, crouch down and crawl through the vent opening on the left. As you approach a grate at the end of the tunnel, you overhear General Standwell talking to Colonel MacCall. Before you break the gate, stop and listen.

CHECKPOINT: FIND GENERAL CARRINGTON'S CELL

Break the grate, then continue down the ventilation shaft until you see an office on the left with a dead Army soldier behind a desk. Break the next grate, and drop down into the room. On the far side of the room is a second desk with a video camera monitoring station. Scout out the hallway with the video camera. Keep watching until you see the soldier with the helmet go back down to the far end of the hallway.

Once the hallway looks clear, switch to the Crossbow and open the door. Zoom in and look down the hallway to the right. After a few seconds the first soldier will walk into view. Pop him in the head with a Crossbow Bolt.

Keep your back to the door, XIII, and the helmet soldier will never notice that you killed one of his buddies.

QUICK AND DIRTY

Climb into the vent, and listen to the conversation.

Exit the vent. Kill the soldiers guarding the hallway, then take the elevator upstairs.

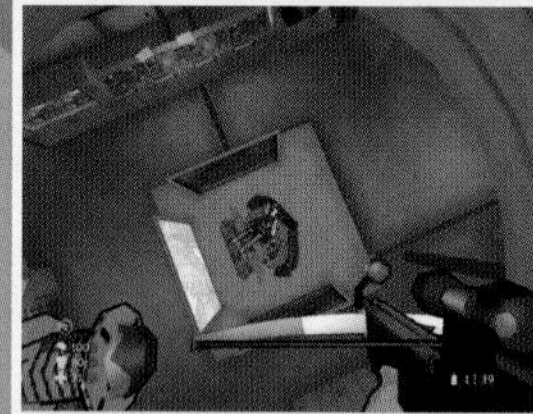

Kill the two soldiers in the upstairs hallway, then climb into the electrical access tunnel next to the locked "ALERT EXIT" door.

Grapple down the electrical shaft, and kill the two soldiers guarding the Magnetic Card. Take the Magnetic Card, kill any soldiers in the hallway, and open the "ALERT EXIT" door.

Eliminate the soldiers in the barracks, then climb through the storage room vent to gain access to General Carrington's cell. Use the Lockpick to free General Carrington.

Kill General Carrington's guard, and protect the general as you flee from the Emerald Army Base.

Continue to watch for a few more seconds and a second soldier will walk into view. Give him a Crossbow Bolt to the head. With that second body lying in plain view, the time for stealth is over. Switch to the Shotgun and get ready for the helmet soldier to come running.

When you see the "Tap, Tap, Tap" of his footsteps, jump out from behind the doorway and give him a couple of quick blasts from the Shotgun. Another soldier comes running from around the corner. Blast him with the Shotgun and he'll go down.

Switch to the Assault Rifle and continue down to the end of the hallway. Just around the last corner is a second helmet soldier. Unload a full clip from the Assault Rifle on him.

Now that you have killed all five soldiers, you can go back and collect weapons and ammo from the bodies. Be sure to search all the rooms for extra goodies. You will find **AR Grenades**, a **Crossbow**, three **MedKits**, a **Light Helmet**, **Light Vest**, **Grenades**, an **Assault Rifle**, a **Shotgun**, plus additional **M16 Ammo** and **Grenades** on the bodies.

There's an elevator where you killed the last soldier. Take a ride up.

As the elevator rises, you will sense that the SPADS soldiers are carrying out General MacCall's orders and eliminating the remaining Army soldiers. When the elevator comes to a stop, exit and head down the hallway.

Make sure your Assault Rifle has a full load of ammo, then walk around the torn-up flooring and the security screen and down the hallway to the left. A single soldier patrols this area. Blast away with the Assault Rifle as you run up to him. If you catch him walking away from you, he won't have time to fire a single shot.

Continue down the hallway, past the "ALERT EXIT" doorway and around the next corner. As you pass the "ALERT EXIT" doorway, be sure to reload your Assault Rifle. Round the next corner and take out the second soldier.

A key card is required to open the "ALERT EXIT" door. If you look through the bulletproof glass windows, you can see a key card on a desk. Go ahead and give those windows a couple of shots; they won't break. Time to find another way into that room, XIII.

There's a stack of crates right next to the "ALERT EXIT" door. Jump up onto the crates, break the grate, and approach the ladder in this access area.

CHECKPOINT: FIND THE KEY CARD

Climb the ladder and make your way through the electrical access tunnel to the next grate. Break the grate and move out onto the ledge. You can see sparks of electricity shooting between terminals in this tunnel.

Attach your Grappling Hook to the hook above you, then look directly down. Wait until the electricity ceases to fire between the terminals and then use Alt-Fire to lower yourself to just above the end of tunnel.

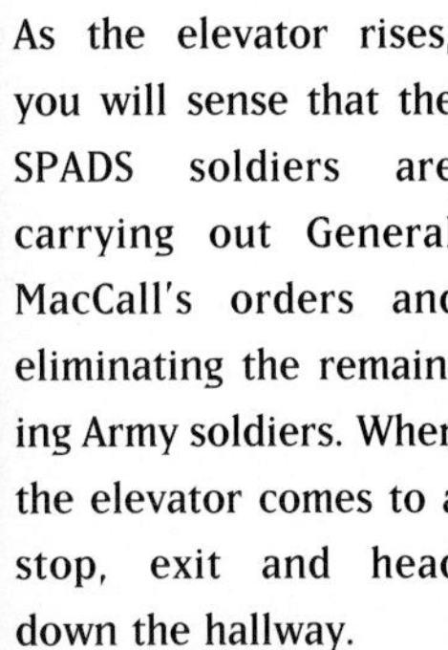

While still attached to the Grappling Hook, equip the Crossbow and shoot the patrolling soldier in the top of the head. A second soldier is walking around the inside of the room on a second floor landing. Quickly lower yourself to the floor, disconnect from the Grappling Hook, and then run and hide behind the bank of computer terminals. The soldier will get off a couple of free shots. Use a **MedKit** to heal yourself back to 100%.

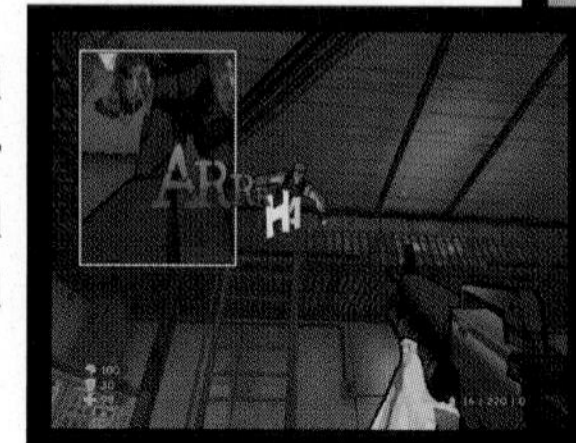

Switch back to the Assault Rifle and sneak along behind the computer terminals until you can get a good shot at the soldier on the second floor landing. Take him out.

Collect the **M16 Ammo** and **Grenades** from the dead bodies. There's also a **MedKit** on a crate in a corner of the room. Go through the small door in the back of the room. As you enter the small office, several soldiers charge forward and try to shoot at you. Good thing for the bulletproof glass. Collect the **Magnetic Card** and the **Grenade**, then exit the room.

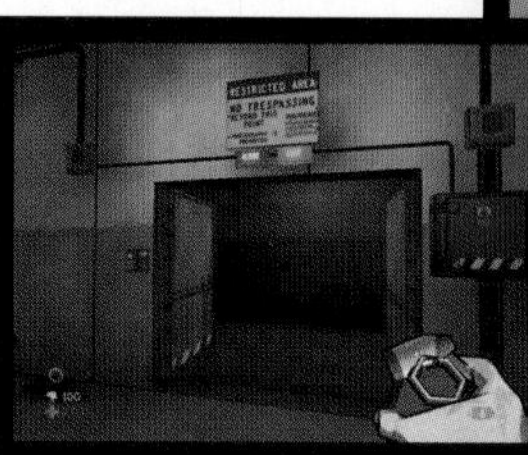

Since you know those three soldiers are waiting just outside the room, use the Magnetic Card to open the door. Switch to a Grenade and toss one out the left side of the door. That should catch one of the three soldiers by surprise.

Head down the hallway and to the left. As you round the first corner, you observe a soldier at the end of the hall near the "ALERT EXIT" door. Kill him with the Assault Rifle or the Crossbow. Use the **Magnetic Card** to open the door.

Behind the "ALERT EXIT" door is a blue-lit room containing computer panels. A single soldier with a Shotgun is in this room monitoring the video camera. Kill him with the Assault Rifle. The noise brings a second helmet soldier to the scene. You should have enough ammo to waste him, too. Collect the **MedKit** and **Shotgun Shells** before you enter the blue computer room.

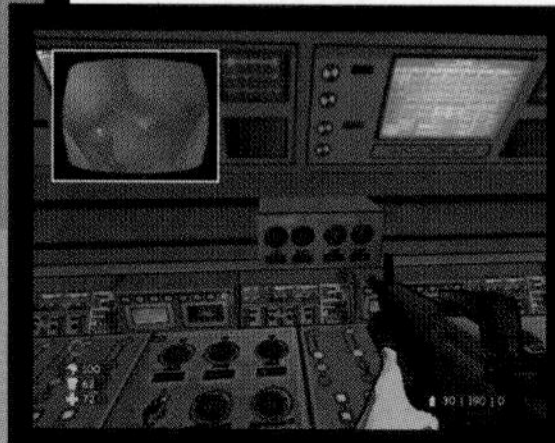

Look at the computer panel the soldier was attending to see General Carrington inside his holding cell.

Enter the hallway and head to the right. There's a restroom behind the door at the end of the hall. Use your Lockpick to open the first stall where you'll find a **Heavy Helmet** and a **Full MedKit**.

Head down the hallway to the right. Note the crushed cigarettes outside two double doors. Open the doors and kill the three soldiers inside. Search this barracks to find a **9mm**, **Shotgun**, **Grenades**, **AR Grenades**, and a **MedKit**. Frisk the bodies for additional Ammo and Armor.

Head back out into the hallway and through the door at the end of the hallway. Pick up the **MedKit**, then climb the crates in the storage room and break the grate. As you climb through the grate, you hear General Carrington's voice. This triggers another flashback.

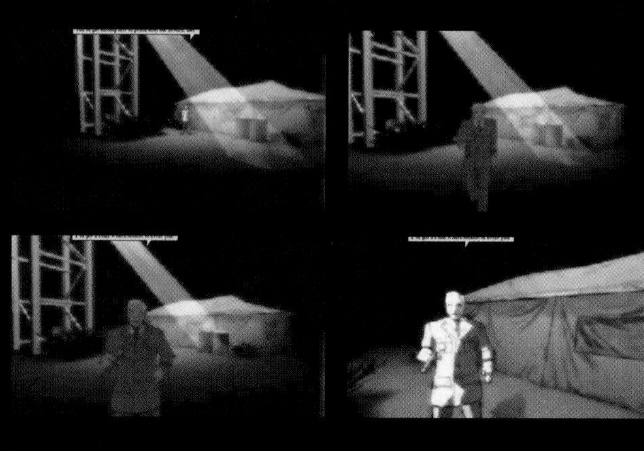

Break the grate at the end of the vent and drop down into the cellblock. Use the **Lockpick** to free General Carrington. Pick up the **Heavy Vest** and the **Full Medkit**.

General Carrington recovers his cigars, and then lures a soldier into the room. After you kill that guy, General Carrington runs out into the hallway. Follow him and eliminate any soldiers you encounter as you escape the base. Watch your back!

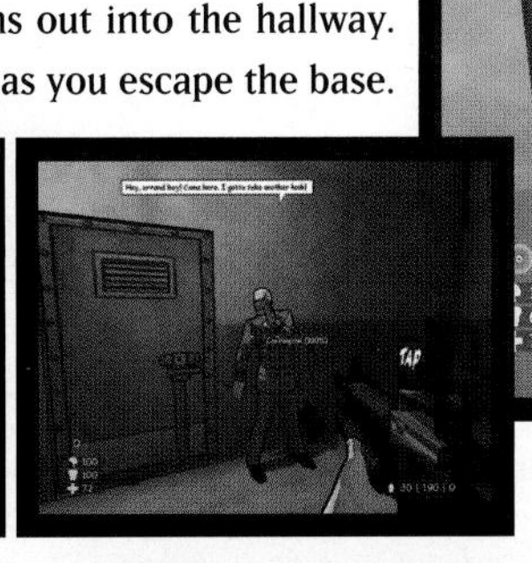

MISSION COMPLETE

Mission 9: ESCAPE THE EMERALD ARMY BASE

QUICK AND DIRTY

Eliminate the three soldiers patrolling outside while General Carrington hides.

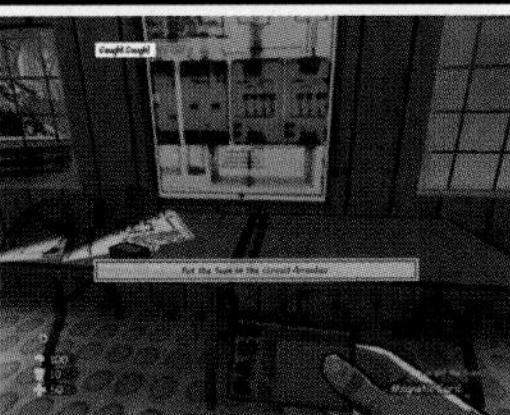

Enter the main cable-car building and kill the three soldiers inside. Collect the Magnetic Card.

Use the Magnetic Card to open the storage building and collect the cable-car fuse. Protect General Carrington from the three soldiers who attack outside.

Put the fuse in the fuse box, then go up onto the roof and throw the cable-car switch. Join General Carrington at the cable-car entrance.

Kill the last two soldiers and join General Carrington in the cable-car.

MISSION BRIEFING

OBJECTIVES

Use the cable-car to leave the base.
General Carrington must not die.

WEAPONS

Assault Rifle	AR Grenades
Sniper Rifle	Grenades

ENEMIES

Soldiers

SUMMARY

Time for a daring escape, XIII. Restore power to the cable-car and make your way down the mountain to where Jones is waiting with a helicopter.

CHECKPOINT: FIND THE FUSE

Follow General Carrington around the side of the fence, XIII. He will stop behind the snow covered trees to brief Jones. Just ahead is the cable-car building and a smaller storage building on the right. You can see two guards patrolling in front of the cable-car building, and a third guard patrolling a gate off to the left.

Switch to the crossbow and keep watch from a distance. The two soldiers in front of the cable-car building walk away from each other toward the ends of the building and back. When the soldier on the right passes in front of the windows and turns his back to you, let him have it with a crossbow bolt to the back of the head.

Ignore the soldier on the right and move off to the left where there are some targets. Use the crossbow to eliminate the soldier in front of the gate. The third soldier is wearing a heavy helmet, so taking spearing him with a crossbow is a no-go. Switch to the Assault Rifle, then move in close behind the stack of snow-covered sandbags and let him have it.

Collect the Ammo and Armor from the dead soldiers to get a **Light Vest** and **AR Ammo**, then head to the right hand side of the cable-car building and break out a window. Jump through and collect the **MedKit**.

A solitary soldier awaits through the next door. Kill him and collect a second **MedKit**. There's a fuse box on the wall with one missing fuse.

Go down the hall. Open the door and you see another soldier patrolling. Use an AR Grenade to blast him from a distance, then enter the cable-car room and waste the second soldier. Collect the **Magnetic Card** from the body.

Exit the front door and head over to the small storage building. Use the **Magnetic Card** to open the door, then collect the **MedKit** and the **Fuse**. General Carrington joins you as soon as you have the Fuse.

Once you step outside, three soldiers come running. Take out the first soldier with the Assault Rifle, then use an AR Grenade to eliminate the other two. Follow General Carrington to the front of the cable-car building.

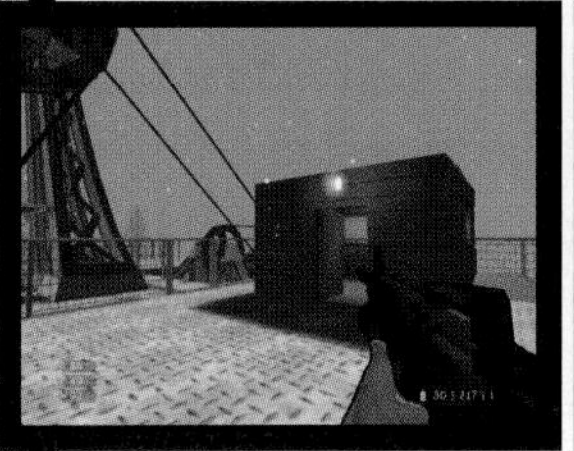

Enter the cable-car building and place the **Fuse** in the Fuse box, then ascend the stairs to the roof on the right side of the building. The cable-car control center is inside a room on the roof. Throw the switch to bring the cable-car up, then join General Carrington in front of the cable-car.

Watch out, XIII! A pair of soldiers attack as soon as you join General Carrington. Kill them with the Assault Rifle, and then collect their **M16 Ammo**, **Light Vest**, and **Light Helmet**. After completing chalking up these casualties, General Carrington has a present for you—the **Sniper Rifle**!

Join General Carrington inside the cable-car to end the mission.

MISSION COMPLETE

Mission 10: ESCORT CARRINGTON TO JONES'S HELICOPTER

MISSION BRIEFING

OBJECTIVES

Use the cable-car to leave the base.
General Carrington must not die.

WEAPONS

Assault Rifle	AR Grenades
Sniper Rifle	Grenades

ENEMIES

Soldiers

SUMMARY

Ready for a nice safe cable-car ride down the mountain, XIII? It's never that easy. Prepare to fend off rocket attacks from the SPADS soldiers, and get General Carrington to Jones's helicopter.

QUICK AND DIRTY

SPADS soldiers attack the cable-car with a RPG (Rocket Propelled Grenade). Use the Sniper Rifle to take out the three SPADS soldiers next to the troop transport trucks.

General Carrington bails out of the cable-car. After you eliminate the soldiers, climb up the ladder and use the Grappling Hook to lower yourself to the ground.

Protect General Carrington from the three SPADS soldiers who attack, then follow the general into the woods.

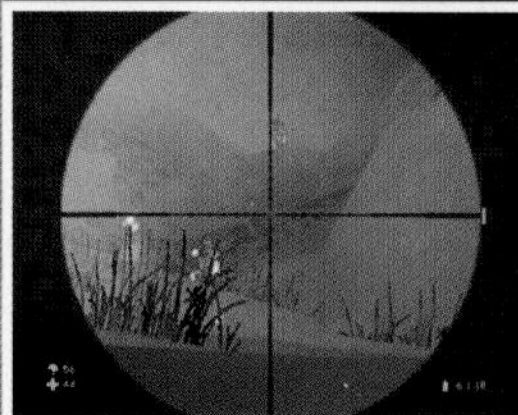

Fight off two more attacks from RPG soldiers and Assault Rifle soldiers as you escort General Carrington through the woods.

Kill the last two soldiers as you climb up the hill to where Jones is waiting with the helicopter.

Carrington and Jones start the chopper while you man the stationary M60 Machine Gun to delay the incoming ground troops.

Once the chopper starts, climb aboard.

As the mission begins, the cable-car comes under attack from an **RPG** (Rocket Propelled Grenade). Smashed and useless, the cable-car swings precariously above the snow swept ground hundreds of feet below. General Carrington bails out, leaving you to cover his escape.

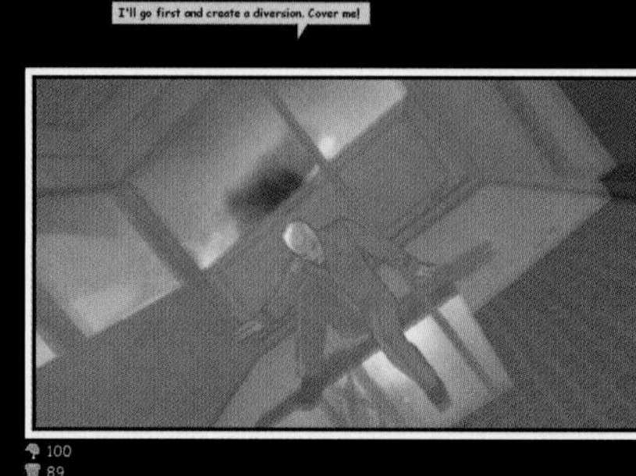

Use the **Sniper Rifle** to eliminate the three SPADS soldiers next to the troop transport trucks. Once they're dead, climb onto the roof of the cable-car and attach your **Grappling Hook** to the yellow and black hook. Just as you do this, the cable snaps and the cable-car crashes to the ground.

Lower yourself to the ground where General Carrington waits.

CHECKPOINT: COVER CARRINGTON

As soon as you hit the ground, two SPADS soldiers attack with Assault Rifles. Use your own trusty Assault Rifle to wipe them out. General Carrington calls out to you, "RPG, 12 o'clock." Take cover beside the general and switch to the **Sniper Rifle**.

Headshot! Peg the RPG soldier up next to the troop transport trucks. General Carrington runs back to a cave in the mountainside and takes cover. Follow him there. Three more soldiers attack when you reach the general's hiding place. Switch back to the Assault Rifle and take them out.

Once the coast is clear the General runs off into the woods to the left. Follow him. Kill the soldier on the overhang as you run into the woods. The General stops and signals that there is another **RPG** soldier up ahead. Switch to the **Sniper Rifle** and nail the RPG soldier and the Assault Rifle soldier.

Follow General Carrington further into the woods until he comes to a stop. Watch out! Two SPADS soldiers are next to a winter camouflage Tank on an overhang behind you. Blast them both with a **Grenade**.

The General continues running uphill until you see Jones. Take out the last two soldiers with your Assault Rifle, and Jones joins you and the general.

The helicopter engine is having problems turning over during the heavy blizzard. General Carrington and Jones head back to the helicopter and try to start it, leaving you behind to delay the attacking SPADS soldiers. Run up to the stationary mounted **M60 Machine Gun** and hit Action.

Use the M60 Machine Gun to mow down the waves of attacking SPADS soldiers while Jones and General Carrington start the helicopter. When the propeller begins to whirl, Jones calls for you to get in. Hit Action again to stop using the M60 Machine Gun, then run around to the back of the helicopter to end the mission.

MISSION COMPLETE

Mission 11:
FIND THE CHALET.

MISSION BRIEFING

OBJECTIVES

Make your way through the snowy woods until you find the chalet. A mysterious woman taking refuge there has clues to your past.

WEAPONS

Double Barrel Shotgun
Shotgun
44 Special
Mini-Gun

ENEMIES

Thugs
Hunters

SUMMARY

Thugs with 44 Special's and Hunters with Double Barrel Shotguns search the frozen woods looking for the hidden chalet and a mysterious woman. Listen for the voices to find your way through the forest.

QUICK AND DIRTY

Head off to the right until you hear thugs and hunters talking. When they move out, kill them with the Double Barrel Shotgun.

Keep moving through the woods until you see two boats. When the red boat speeds off, kill the two thugs.

Move into the woods until you hear more hunters and thugs building a snowman out of an unfortunate hiker. Kill them, then head down to the water's edge.

Jump from one ice flow to the next to cross the water. Kill two thugs who attack as you head up the last chunk of ice, then jump back onto the land.

Kill the lone thug at the top of the hill and move toward a stand of fallen trees. Prepare to be ambushed by five thugs.

Walk along the river's edge and cross it at the waterfall, then kill the last thug behind you and make your way through the woods until you see the chalet.

CHECKPOINT: TREK THROUGH THE WOODS

Jones drops you off in the woods near the chalet. Venture deeper into the forest just to the right of the large stone outcropping. After a short walk you will overhear several thugs and hunters talking about trying to find the cabin. When they stop talking, two of them come around the trees toward you.

Switch to the Double Barrel Shotgun and blow away the first two thugs. The noise brings the second pair running. Quickly hit Action to reload and take out these guys, as well. Collect the **44 Special** ammo, **Cal 12** ammo, and **MedKit** from the dead bodies, and then continue into the woods.

Stay to the right until you hear some more thugs talking. Move left a bit into a stand of trees. At the bottom of the hill, you will see two boats. Once they spot you, the red boat speeds off and the two thugs attack. Try hitting them from a distance with the **44 Special**. Once they're dead, go down the hill and grab the **Full MedKit** from the dark green boat.

Keep to the right as you continue your wilderness trek. When you approach the top of the hill, you will overhear some thugs talking about making a snowman. Use the **44 Special** to quickly obliterate all three of them. A fourth thug armed with a Shotgun waits on the other side of the clearing, but a couple of shots from the 44 Special and he will cease to be a problem. A shame about that poor hiker.

As you move past the grisly snowman, a hunter armed with a Double Barrel Shotgun attacks from behind a tree. Dispatch him and move uphill. A broken down cabin and a frozen hiker are the next points of interest at the precipice. Jones radios that the cabin is on the other side of the waterfall. Collect the **Full MedKit** from the cabin, then head back down the hill.

A thug armed with a MiniGun runs at you shooting. A quick double tap from the **44 Special** is in order here. Collect his **MiniGun**, then follow the path past the snowman and down a pathway on the left side that leads to the water's edge.

Jump from one ice flow to the next until you reach the largest frozen chunk. As you climb to the edge you will see two thugs across the water. Take them out with some **44 Special** shots, then leap to the shore.

CHECKPOINT: AMBUSH IN THE WOODS

Climb the hill and head to the right. From a railing at the top, you will see a single thug armed with a Double Barrel Shotgun. Since he has his back to you, move up behind him and blow him away with your own **Double Barrel Shotgun**.

You also hear voices from just ahead. When you reach the place where a fallen tree leans against the ice, you will be surrounded by five thugs. It's an ambush, XIII!

Switch to the regular **Shotgun** and use the trees for cover as you blast the opposition away. Beware of the thug up on the rocks. After you take care of your surprise party, collect all the ammo before you head off to the waterfall.

Make your crossing at the base of the waterfall and follow the ledge on the river bank. You will suddenly sense an attacker from behind! Use the **44 Special** to eliminate the last thug up on a large rock across the river. Keep moving down the path until you see the chalet at the bottom of the hill.

MISSION COMPLETE

Mission 12: CABIN IN THE WOODS.

MISSION BRIEFING

OBJECTIVES

Talk to Kim Rowland. Cover Kim's escape from the chalet.

WEAPONS

- 44 Special
- Shotgun
- Double Barrel Shotgun
- MiniGun
- M60 MachineGun

ENEMIES

Thugs

SUMMARY

Once you reach the chalet and talk to Kim Rowland, you learn and more about your missing identity, XIII. When the chalet comes under attack, fend off the enemy with the M60 Machine Gun while Kim makes her escape.

QUICK AND DIRTY

Find the chalet in the woods. Looks familiar, doesn't it?

Talk to Kim Rowland to trigger an extended flashback sequence.

Get the M60 Machine Gun from the secret hiding place and fight off dozens of thugs while Kim Roland escapes though the back of the cabin.

When the attack stops, make your way out the back of the cabin to find Jones and Carrington.

Avalanche!

CHECKPOINT: FIND THE CHALET

A short march through the woods leads you right to the cabin's front door. Inside, Kim Rowland talks to you, triggering a flashback.

CHECKPOINT: COVER KIM'S ESCAPE

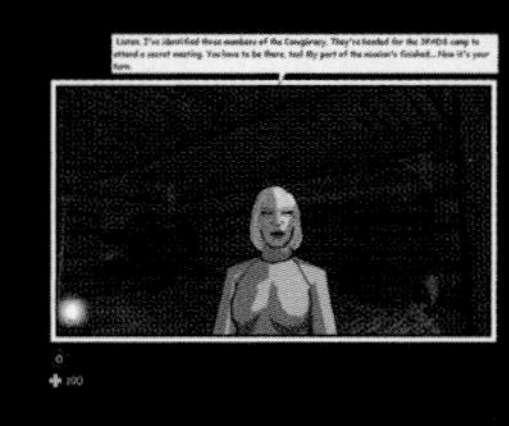

The cabin is under attack, XIII. Quickly grab the **M60 Machine Gun** from the secret hiding place. On the shelf next to the hiding place is **5.56 Ammo**, **M60 Ammo**, **12 Gauge Ammo**, a **Light Vest**, **Heavy Helmet**, and a **MedKit**. There's also a **Full MedKit** on the destroyed bed.

Dozens of thugs, including some armed with RPG rockets, assault the cabin. Shoot out the windows and use the openings to target the enemies outside. Stay inside the cabin, as it offers substantial protection from the RPGs.

A helicopter will hover low over the cabin as thugs shoot at you from inside. Step outside and let the helicopter have it with the **M60 Machine Gun**. Take cover inside the cabin after the helicopter is destroyed.

CHECKPOINT: FIND JONES & CARRINGTON AGAIN

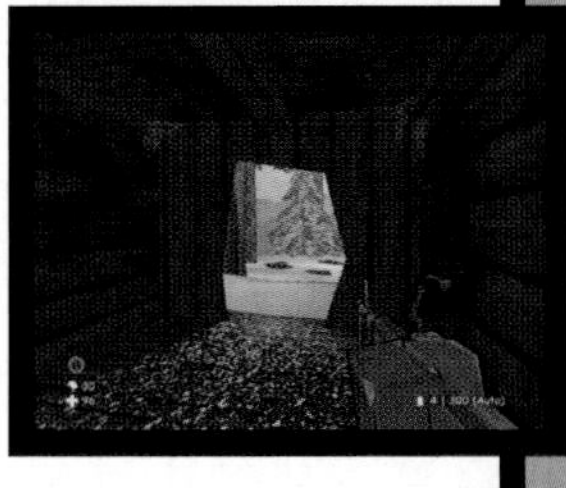

Once the assault from the front of the cabin stops, an RPG attack destroys the rear of this rustic dwelling. Head out back and kill any thugs you find. There's extra **M60 Ammo** and a **MedKit** in the outhouse.

Start heading down the mountain to rendezvous with Jones and Carrington in the helicopter. The thugs aren't going out quietly. An RPG attack comes from behind you, aimed up at the mountain. Moments later, a couple thousand tons of snow and ice begin a treacherous descent down the slopes. Avalanche!

MISSION COMPLETE

Mission 13:

CAPTURED

MISSION BRIEFING

OBJECTIVES

Escape from custody.

WEAPONS

44 Special
Shotgun
Double Barrel Shotgun
MiniGun
M60 Machine Gun

ENEMIES

Prison Guards

SUMMARY

Out of the frying pan and into the fire, XIII. You awake from the avalanche to find yourself the unwelcome guest of Doctor Johansson. Escape from custody before you find yourself next in line for his special treatments.

QUICK AND DIRTY

After Dr. Johansson has a little chat with you, follow the guards downstairs to the laundry room.

Knock out the two guards and take the storage room key. Open the storage room and climb up to the vent.

Use the vents to cross the room to a second vent. Collect the Throwing Knives, then head into the ventilation shaft.

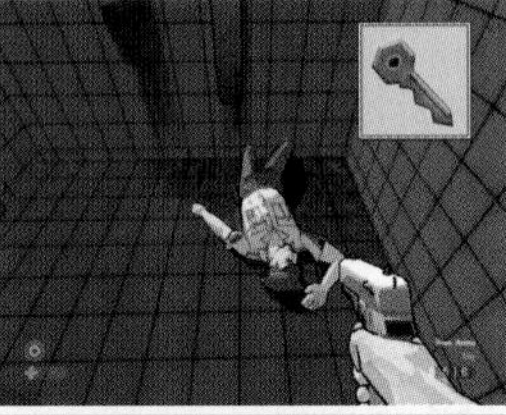

Kill the single security guard inside the guardroom and take his 9mm and Key. Eliminate the two guards in the hallway outside and take their Keys.

Head upstairs to the cellblock and unlock the doors leading upstairs.

Kill the security guard behind the locked gate and collect his Key. Waste two more security guards at the end of the hall. Kill the three security guards on the second floor, then unlock the gate.

Collect the Sniper Rifle from the storage room and take the elevator upstairs. Use the Sniper Rifle to kill the four security guards upstairs.

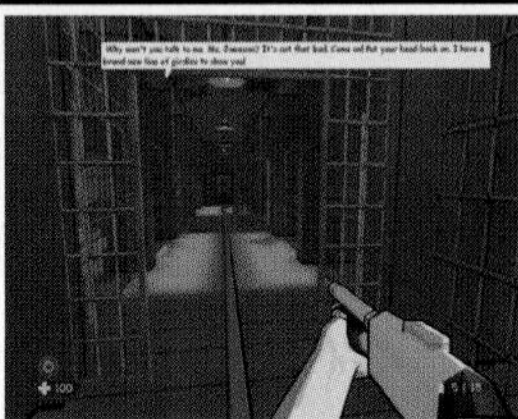

Use the Shotgun to kill the security guard in the electrocution chamber, then head down the cellblock to the electrical access tunnel.

Kill the escaped lunatic. Climb down the ladder to the sewage tunnel, and then back up the next ladder to end the mission.

CHECKPOINT: TRAPPED WITH THE LOONY

When you regain consciousness, you find yourself the cellmate of a SPADS soldier who has gone stark raving mad. While his observations are amusing, they don't help you escape. After a few minutes, the good doctor arrives with two security guards and suggests that you be taken out of your cell and cleaned up.

CHECKPOINT: CRUEL & UNUSUAL PUNISHMENT

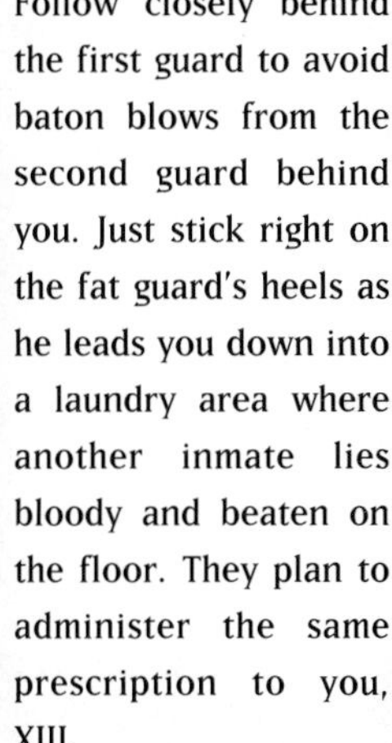

Follow closely behind the first guard to avoid baton blows from the second guard behind you. Just stick right on the fat guard's heels as he leads you down into a laundry area where another inmate lies bloody and beaten on the floor. They plan to administer the same prescription to you, XIII.

Grab one of the **bottles** on the table, and then smack the uniformed security guard with it when he tries to attack you. Grab a second bottle and take out the next guard, then collect the **Supply Closet Key** from one of the guards.

Open the supply closet in the back of the room with your new key. Use your fists to crush some of the cardboard boxes stacked inside the supply closet, and then climb up to a ventilation grate.

Smash the grate and make your way through the vent, then knock open the next grate.

Nice view from up here, XIII. Climb along the top of the ventilation shafts to the other side of the room. You must jump from one vent to the next to cross the room. You'll find some **Throwing Knives** inside one of the vents. Smash the next grate to enter the vent that leads to the room with the single guard.

From up here you can easily take out the security guard below with a single Throwing Knife to the head. Jump off the right side of the vent and onto the top of some cabinets, then onto the floor. Snag the **9mm** off the table and the **Door Key** from the guard's body.

Open the door and plug the two brown shirt security guards with the 9mm. Each guard has a Key, and you need both of them. Head back up the stairs to the cellblock. You can use your Keys to get back into the cellblock and some of the cells. Search around until you locate the **Full MedKit**.

When you obtain it, use your keys to unlock the doors and leave the cellblock. Time to go upstairs.

CHECKPOINT: ESCAPE FROM THE HIGH-SECURITY AREA

There is one brown shirt security guard with a 9mm pistol behind a locked gate. Shoot him through the bars, then unlock the gate. Collect his **Key** and **9mm Ammo**. Two more brown shirt security guards start shooting at you from the far end of the hallway.

Dodge into the side hallways as you head to the next locked gate. Shoot through the gate and kill the two more brown shirt security guards. Three green shirt security guards with Shotguns are up on the second level. Keep shooting through the gate until you have killed these three guards, as well. Use your Key to unlock the gate.

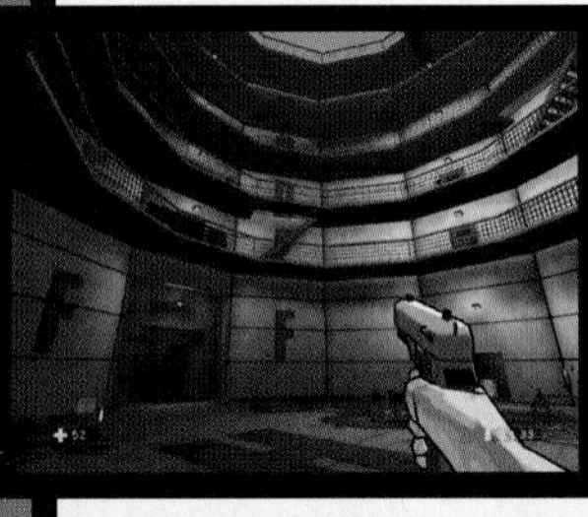

There's a **MedKit** in a storage closet on the right side of the room. You'll also find the **Sniper** Rifle, 12 Cal Ammo, and a **Grenade** in a storage closet on the left side of the room. Collect additional **9mm Ammo** from the dead security guards.

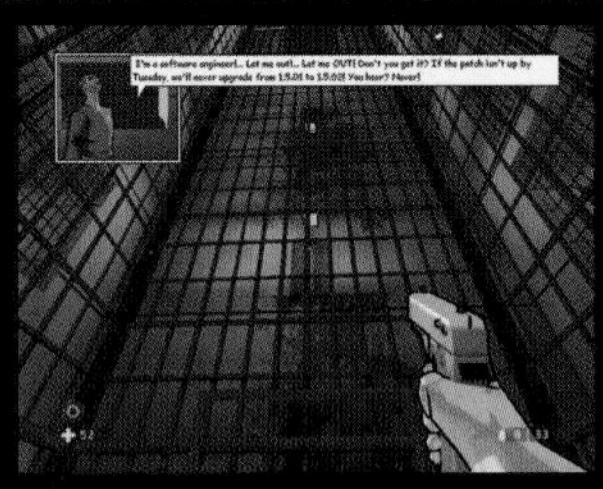

Unlock the next gate and take the elevator upstairs. Software development must be rough, XIII—a mental patient is screaming about patch files as you head upstairs.

Once the elevator gate opens, switch to the **Sniper Rifle** and wait until you see the first guard walk by, then bring him down. This alerts several other security guards, including one in the tower straight ahead. You can shoot through the bars and take out three more security guards.

Switch to the **Shotgun** and exit the gate on the left. There's a single security guard with a Shotgun behind the closed door. He runs and hides behind the door when you open it. A quick blast from the Shotgun takes him out. Collect his **12 Gauge Ammo**.

Make your way past the electrocution chair and down the "Red Mile." A single cell is open and an unconscious security guard lies on the floor.

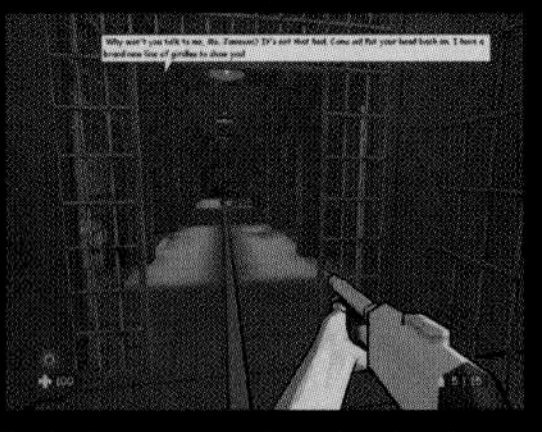

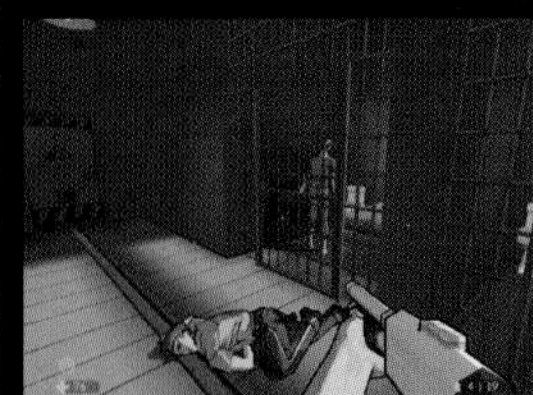

Did someone escape?

Duck down and enter the electrical access tunnel. Before you exit the tunnel, watch for the "Tap, Tap, Tap" of the footsteps of the escaped mental patient. Shoot him when you exit the tunnel and collect more **9mm Ammo**.

An open tunnel with a ladder leads underground. Start climbing down. Whoops! It's a bit slippery. Don't worry, when you fall you will land in some water. Swim over to the next ladder and start climbing to end the mission.

MISSION COMPLETE

Mission 14:

THE DOCTOR IS IN!

MISSION BRIEFING

OBJECTIVES

Find a way to get out of the asylum.
Do not kill the medical staff.

WEAPONS

Throwing Knife	Shotgun
9mm	Sniper Rifle
9mm Silencer	Grenades
44 Special	

ENEMIES

Hospital Guards
Dr. Johansson

SUMMARY

Exploratory surgery is not on your schedule, XIII. You need to find a way to escape the asylum without killing any of the medical staff. Watch out for Dr. Johansson; he has plans of his own.

QUICK AND DIRTY

Go out into the hallway and listen in on the medical staff until a security guard opens a door behind you. Kill him and take his **Magnetic Key**.

Sneak past the front desk nurse and open the double doors with the Magnetic Key. Kill the guard across the hall to arm yourself with a 44 Special.

Run down the long hallway, killing all the security guards that you see. Eliminating them quickly keeps them from sounding the alarm and summoning extra help.

Go through the incinerator room into the Lab. Jump up on top of the morgue cabinet to crawl into a vent.

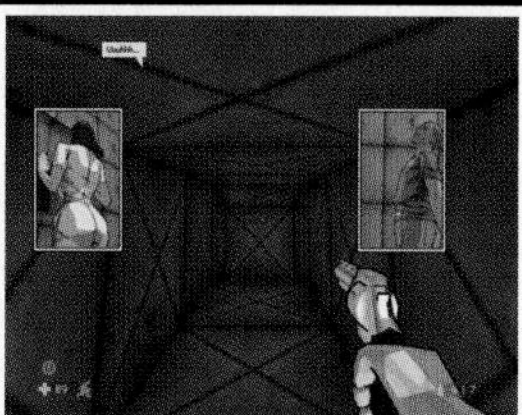

Make your way through the vent and across the ceiling tiles until you fall into Dr. Johansson's lab.

Fight Doctor Johansson!

Take the nurse hostage. Make your way back to the front desk where the front desk nurse will open the outside doors. Take the ambulance and escape the asylum.

CHECKPOINT: LAVATORY OF FEAR

The sewage pipe leads up into an empty restroom. Exit through the door and head down the hallway to the right. You will see one of the staff doctors heading through a double door with a magnetic lock. Without a key card you can't open this door, XIII.

One door in this hallway opens into a monitoring station with four cameras you can use to scope out the asylum hallways. There is a **MedKit** here.

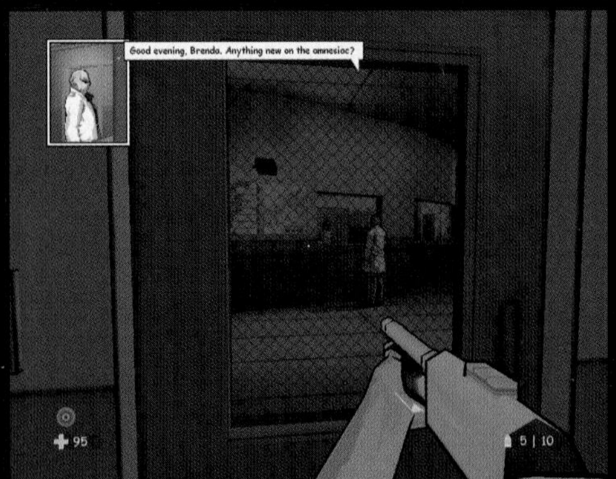

After getting the lay of the land from the camera system, go out the next door and head down the hall to another door with a magnetic lock. You can see one of the medical staff talking to the desk nurse. He is getting ready to head home for the day. Listen in on their conversation until a hospital guard emerges from a side door behind you.

Head back down the hallway until you see the hospital guard behind an open door. He has his back turned, so kill him with the Shotgun and collect the **9mm Silencer** and the **Magnetic Card**.

Return to the single door with the magnetic lock and use the **Magnetic Card** to open the door. Crouch down and wait until the desk nurse has her back to you. Make your way across the room, then use the Magnetic Card while still crouched to open the double doors.

Open the first door across from the magnetic double doors. A single security guard is inside this room. Switch to the **Silenced 9mm** and kill him with a couple of quick head shots. Collect the **44 Special** and **9mm Ammo** from the desk.

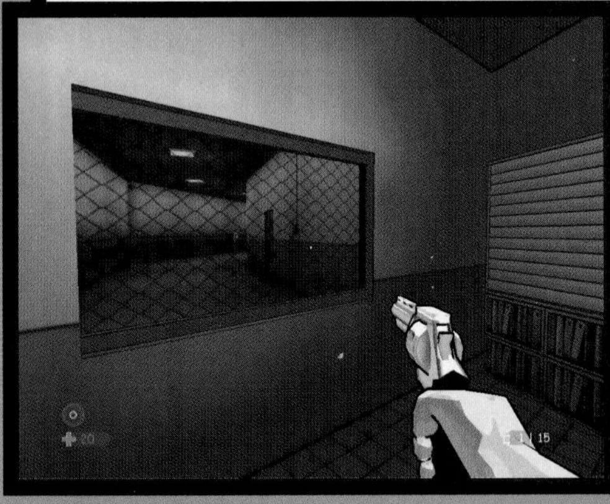

From this room, you can see down a long hallway with security guards every few feet. There are alarm boxes on the walls. If a guard sets one, several extra guards armed with Shotguns will show up as reinforcements.

Go out into the hallway and up to the double doors leading into the long hallway. After a few seconds, a security guard exits the first door and sees you standing behind the double doors. This is your chance, XIII.

Switch to the **44 Special** and run down the hallway, using head shots from the 44 Special to take out the first two guards before they can hit the alarm. Continue your dash through the hall, shooting all the guards with the 44 Special, then stop when you reach the double doors at the end of the hallway.

A member of the hospital staff runs out of a side door behind you and hits the alarm. Too late for that, since you've already taken care of all the guards who would respond to such an alert. Open the last door in this hallway and collect the **MedKit** and **Full MedKit** from the storage room.

Go through the double doors at the end of the hall and head straight ahead for Dr. Johansson's office. It's secured with a magnetic lock. Just what is he doing in there? Go into the incinerator room and exit the next door into the hallway.

Just up ahead you can hear a doctor and a nurse complaining about the smell from the morgue. Enter the lab and they will both raise their arms and surrender. Do not kill them. Instead, knock them out with a chair and collect the **Full MedKit**.

Two security guards armed with Shotguns then run into the hall and start shooting at you. Kill them both with the 44 Special and grab their **12 Gauge Ammo**, then go back into the lab and open the mortuary cabinet door. Gross!

With the morgue cabinet door open, you can jump up onto the top of the cabinet, break the ventilation shaft grate, and climb into the vent.

CHECKPOINT: THE GOOD DOCTOR

As you crawl through the vent, you hear a nurse screaming to be released from a cell where she has been trapped with a psychopath. Keep moving through the vent until you reach the ceiling above Dr. Johansson's lab.

Move carefully across the ceiling panels. You will hear Dr. Johansson in his lab conducting some experiments on an unsuspecting patient. Just past where you can find a window looking down into the lab, the ceiling panels will collapse!

The Doctor is in, XIII. On the agenda for today is a lesion in dissection. Save yourself and attack the doctor!

BOSS FIGHT: DOCTOR JOHANSSON

The Doctor moves very fast. He uses throwing knives as his main weapon, and will jab you with a needle full of a hallucinogenic drug if he gets close. You will drop your weapon if he stabs you with that needle.

Try to keep the dead patient between you and the doctor, and keep moving at all times. When Doctor Johansson runs out of throwing knives, he will grab some chemicals from a rack in the back of the room and start throwing them like Grenades.

The **Shotgun** or **44 Special** works best against this guy. Remember to reload often and use your **MedKits** if your health starts getting low.

Once the doctor is dead, take his **Key**. Search the room for extra **Throwing Knives**, a **MedKit**, and a **Full MedKit**. The nurse trapped in a room off to the side will beg you to let her out, but you don't have the Key. Head over to Doctor Johansson's desk and pick up another **MedKit**.

The picture on the wall triggers a flashback. The Sanctuary...

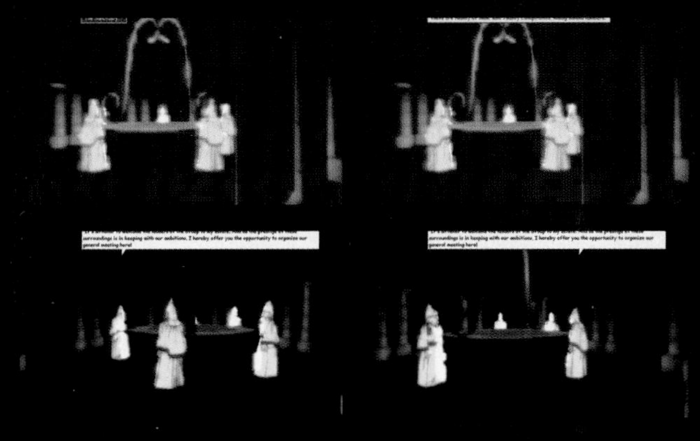

After the flashback, the picture on the wall slides aside to reveal a wall safe. Use Doctor Johansson's key to open the safe and recover your **Lockpick**, **Hook**, **Transmitter**, and the **Cell Key**.

Open the cell and free the nurse. There's another **MedKit** and a **Full MedKit** inside the cell. As soon as the nurse comes out the security guards will locate you again. Take the nurse hostage to prevent the security guards from shooting at you.

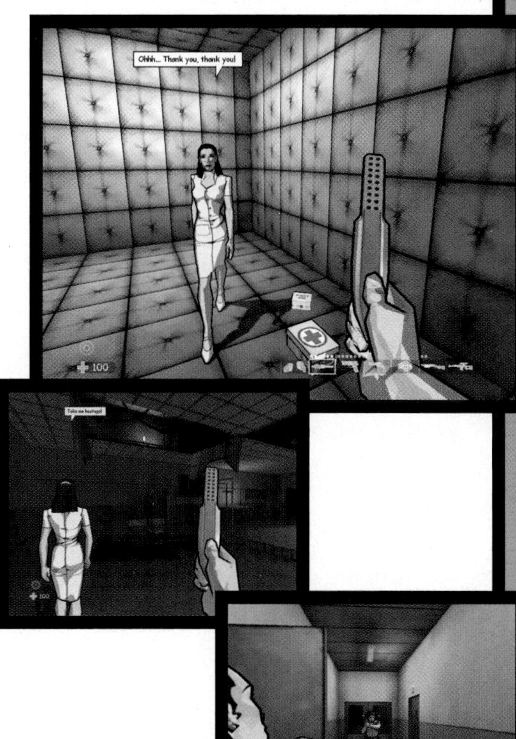

You can still use weapons while you have a hostage, but you can't reload. Make sure all your weapons are fully loaded before you take the nurse hostage.

Use those extra Throwing Knives you found to stab the guards as you move slowly back toward the front desk.

Karen will force the front desk nurse to open the door. Kill the last security guard and head out to the ambulance bay to end the mission.

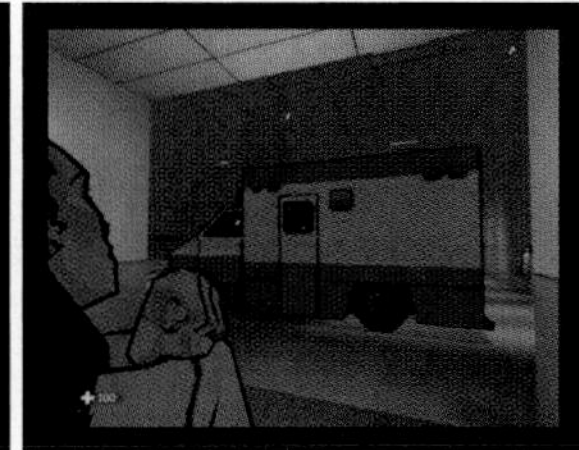

Mission 15:

THE SCENIC ROUTE

MISSION BRIEFING

OBJECTIVES

Find the mine entrance to rejoin Jones.

WEAPONS

44 Special	Sniper Rifle
Shotgun	Bazooka
Kalash	Grenades

ENEMIES

Thugs

SUMMARY

After your narrow escape from the asylum, you need to make your way to where Jones is waiting, XIII. The canyons around Plain Rock are heavily patrolled by thugs—including some armed with deadly Bazooka RPGs. Find the mine entrance to meet up with Jones.

QUICK AND DIRTY

Say goodbye to the nurse and use the Hook to climb up into the canyons. Kill the first five thugs you encounter, and then use the Hook to scale another cliff.

Kill the three thugs armed with Bazookas, as well as the next pair as you climb up the cliff edge and cross the two stone bridges.

Kill three more thugs, then ride the mining cable across the canyon. Make your way down the cliff edge and through a short tunnel.

Dodge more Bazooka Rockets, then kill the three thugs and make your way up the side of the canyon to the mining ruins.

Survive a helicopter attack, then ride the mining cables across the canyon. Kill the two thugs up there and ride the next wire across another long canyon.

Kill the thug at the bottom of the cliff and grab the Bazooka and Bazooka rockets. Walk up to the stone arch and start firing Rockets at several waves of thugs.

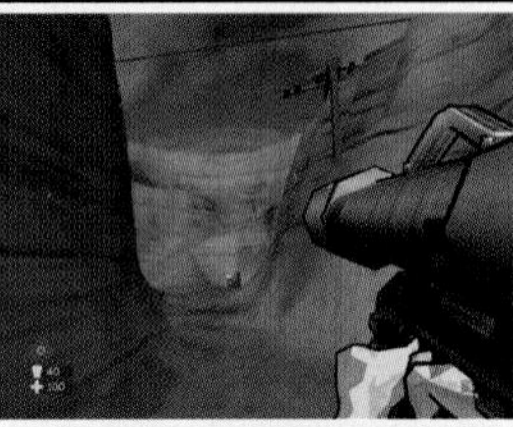

Walk along the canyon floor until you can see more thugs at the end of the canyon. Blast them with Bazooka Rockets, then climb the cliff edge to the top of the canyon.

Kill two more thugs and ride the wire across to the mine entrance. Collect the Important Document at the bottom of the mine, behind some boards, then exit the canyon through the other mine tunnel.

CHECKPOINT: GOING OFF-ROAD

Bid farewell to the nurse who helped you escape from Pain Rock, then collect the **Full MedKit** and start off through the canyons.

When you see the hook above you, use the Grappling Hook to pull yourself up the side of the rocks. Switch to the Sniper Rifle and head down the hill. You will see a box of **5.56 Ammo** hidden behind some rocks. From this spot, use the Sniper Rifle to peg the two attacking thugs.

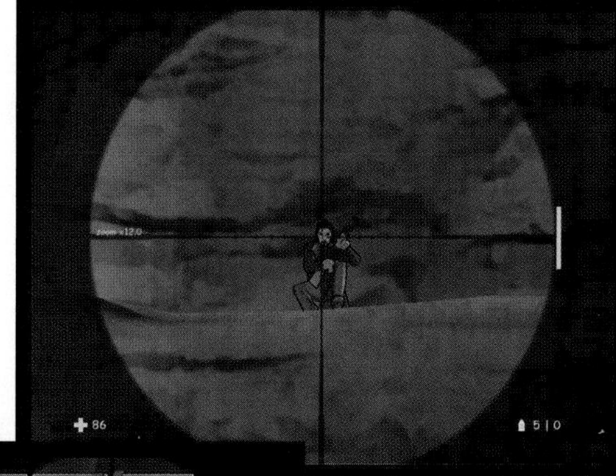

Collect the **44 Ammo**, **Kalash**, and **Grenade** from the first dead thug. Keep moving down the canyons until you see the next hook in the rocks above you. Switch to the Kalash automatic rifle and take out the three thugs who attack you. When they're dead, use the Grappling Hook to pull yourself up to the next area.

One of the Thugs here quickly runs across a stone outcropping and ducks down behind some cover. He keeps popping up and shooting at you, then ducking down quickly. Try using the 44 Special to hit him when he pops his head up out of his hiding spot.

Move down the canyon path until you see the crate with the **Heavy Vest**, **Heavy Helmet** and **MedKit**. Listen to the chatter of the three thugs armed with Bazooka RPGs, then switch to the Sniper Rifle after you collect the body armor.

Look straight down the canyon until you see the first thug walk into view. Plug him with a shot from the Sniper Rifle. After killing the first thug, the others may go into hiding. Switch to the Kalash and move down the canyon until you see the grave markers.

A single thug is crouched down around the corner to the right. Blast him with the Kalash. Keep an eye out on the rocks above for the other two RPG thugs.

If the coast is clear, move up the path to the stone bridges. A single thug armed with a Shotgun attacks you here. Usher him into a similar fate with the Kalash.

Approach the first stone bridge, then jump across to the second one. An RPG thug may start shooting at you from behind, but he shouldn't be able to hit you. Walk up the second stone bridge to the Ammo crate and collect the three **Grenades** and **Cal 12 Ammo**.

CHECKPOINT: FIND THE MINE ENTRANCE

Around the next corner, you can see a broken down mine cart and a cable assembly leading from one side of the canyon to the other. Use the Sniper Rifle to eliminate the two thugs on the other side of the canyon, then hit Action when standing next to the cable assembly to traverse the canyon.

Collect the **BMG50 Ammo** from the dead thug, then walk along the cliff's edge until you can look down into the canyon. There is one thug at the bottom of the canyon with a 44 Special. Shoot him with the Sniper Rifle, then jump down near the mine cart and collect the **Heavy Helmet**, **Heavy Vest**, **Box of BMG50 Ammo**, and **Box of 12 Cal Ammo**.

Climb down to the bottom of the valley, and then duck under the stone bridge with the mine cart. A tunnel leads into the rock on the other side of the stone bridge.

As you see the end of the tunnel, you sense thugs with RPGs up ahead. Wait here for a few seconds until the first thug begins shooting rockets at you. He's up on the canyon edge, right across from the tunnel entrance. Shoot him with the Sniper Rifle.

A second thug is beside some old mining equipment to the right. Pop out of the tunnel entrance and shoot him with the Sniper Rifle. If you miss on the first shot, quickly duck back into the tunnel to avoid being hit with a Bazooka rocket.

The third thug, armed with a 44 Special, is way across the canyon beside another cable assembly. Kill him with the Sniper Rifle, then head down the canyon to the left and collect a **MedKit**.

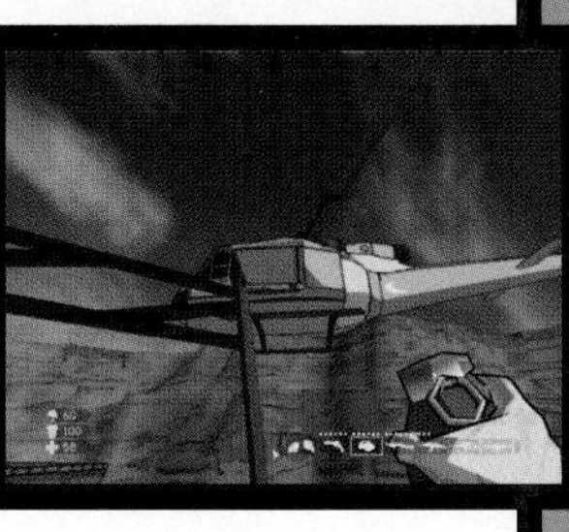

Walk up the ledge to the mining equipment and grab another **MedKit**. When you reach this area, a helicopter flies in close and attacks. Switch to a **Grenade** and hold down Fire to bleed off time until there is only one minute remaining. Let the Grenade fly at the helicopter and blast it out of the sky.

A thug armed with a 44 Special will begin shooting at you from the direction where you just came from. Turn and shoot him with the Sniper Rifle.

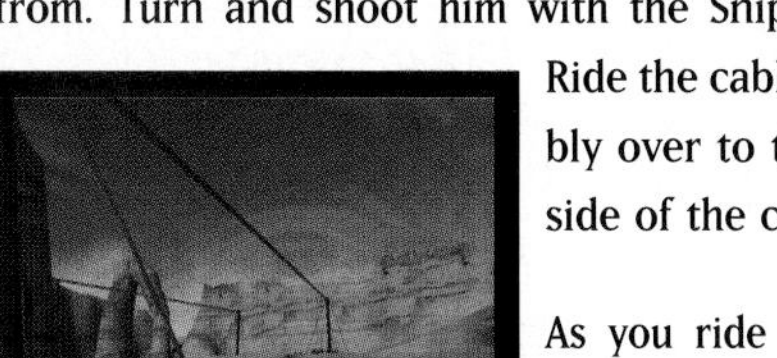

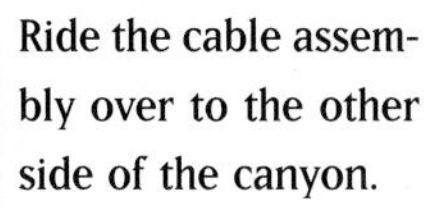

Ride the cable assembly over to the other side of the canyon.

As you ride the wire across, look back and kill the thug waiting on the other side of the canyon, then ride the second wire over to where he was waiting. Collect the **Heavy Vest** and the **Bazooka Rockets**. Ride the same wire back.

Follow the cliff edge off to where there is another wire assembly. Just past the wire is a thug armed with a Kalash. Kill him and collect more **Bazooka Rockets**. Ride the wire across and pick up the **Full MedKit**.

CHECKPOINT: ROCKETS, ROCKETS EVERYWHERE

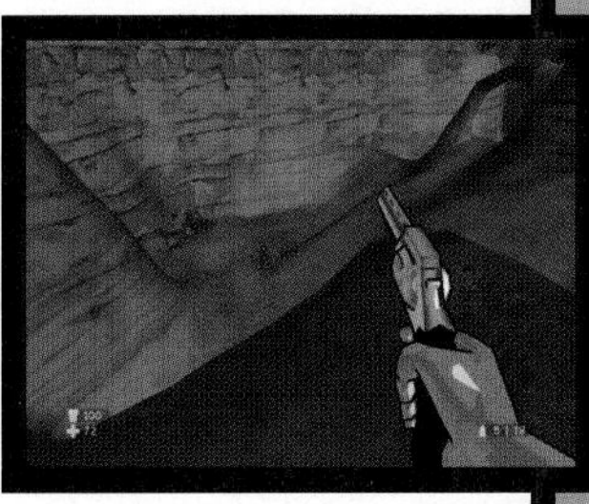

You have been on the receiving end of those Bazooka Rockets long enough, XIII. Time to dish some back. Switch to the **44 Special** and walk toward the edge of the cliff. Down below is a single thug with a Bazooka. Kill him with the 44 Special, then make your way down the cliff to gather the **Bazooka** and **Bazooka Rockets**.

Switch to the Bazooka and walk back up the cliff near a stone arch. Just as you walk under the arch, shoot a Bazooka Rocket down into the bottom of the canyon. You will catch four thugs all at once with that first blast.

Three more waves of thugs come running around the corner after you waste the first four. Keep hammering away at them with Bazooka Rockets until the coast is clear.

Gather up all the ammo from the dead bodies. You will find lots of **44 Ammo** and some extra **Bazooka Rockets**. Walk along the canyon floor and around the corner. You can see more thugs at the end of the canyon. A couple of well-placed Bazooka Rockets will take care of them.

Pick up the **Light Vest** and **Full MedKit** from the Ammo crate, then make your way up the side of the canyon. Decimate the two thugs at the top of the canyon with Bazooka Rockets, then ride the wire at the top of the canyon over to the mine entrance.

Follow the mine car tracks down to the bottom of the mineshaft. Use the Shotgun to break apart some boards, then pick up the **Important Document** off the barrels. Follow the tracks back up to the mine entrance and go up the left-hand passage. Break some boards to complete the mission.

MISSION COMPLETE

Mission 16:
RUINS IN THE ROCKS.

MISSION BRIEFING

OBJECTIVES

Jones has hidden an airplane away. Find it.

WEAPONS

44 Special	Grenades
Shotgun	Throwing Knife
Kalash	9mm
Sniper Rifle	44 Special
Bazooka	Kalash

ENEMIES

Thugs

SUMMARY

Your escape is almost complete, XIII. Make your way across the last of the canyons and past some ancient ruins to where Jones has hidden a jet aircraft.

QUICK AND DIRTY

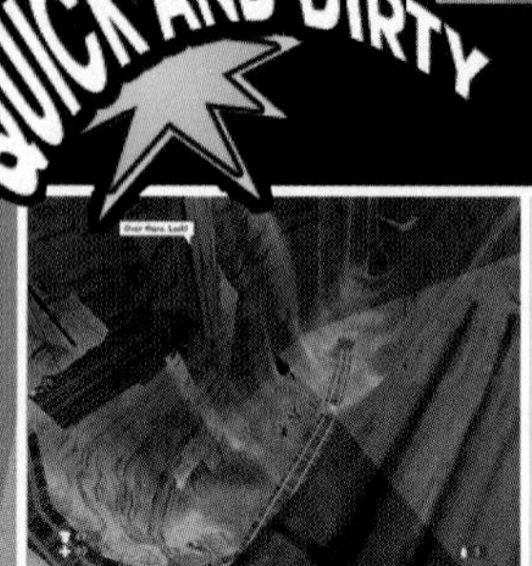

An unwelcoming party is waiting for you at the bottom of the canyon. Say, hello by raining a few Grenades down on them.

Ride the mining cable down to the cliff edge. Collect the MedKit and Bazooka Rockets, then follow the mining cart track down the canyon floor.

Fight off more Bazooka attacks from thugs up in the sides of the canyon. Use the Hook to pull yourself up to the cliff edge.

Fight off more thugs, then jump across the broken stone bridge to the other side of the canyon. Kill the thugs there and in the valley below before climbing down the stone steps to the canyon floor.

Climb the wooden ladders to the ruins. Move along the cliff wall to where you can collect some extra Bazooka Rockets and a Full MedKit. Use the Sniper Rifle to eliminate thugs waiting for you back at the ruins.

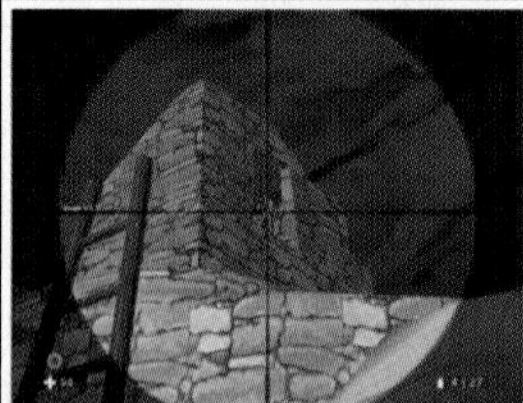

Climb the ladder leading to the ruins and use Bazooka Rockets to take out the thugs shooting down at you from high in the ruins. Collect the MedKits lying on the edge of the ruins.

Go up path on the right side of the ruins, killing any thugs who try to stop you. Climb a ladder inside the ruins to get to the back of the cave.

Inside one of the ruined buildings you will find another thug and a boarded up tunnel entrance. Kill the thug and break the boards with the Shotgun. Make your way through the tunnel to where Jones has hidden an airplane.

One last rocket attack will come from high up on the canyon wall. Kill this enemy, then use the airplane to escape the canyons.

CHECKPOINT: MINE ENTRANCE

Exit the mine to a platform at the top of the canyon. Take a peek over the edge to spy four thugs at the bottom of the canyon. Rain two or three Grenades down on them.

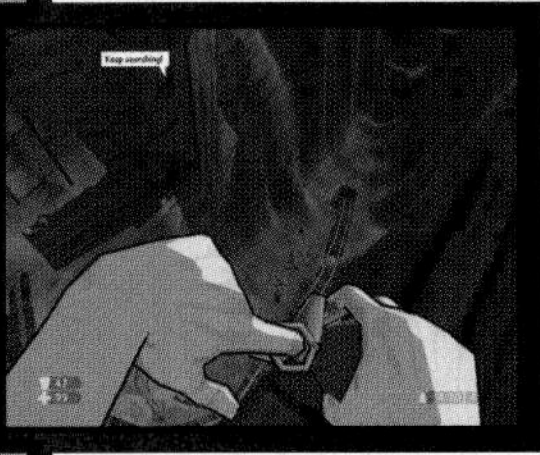

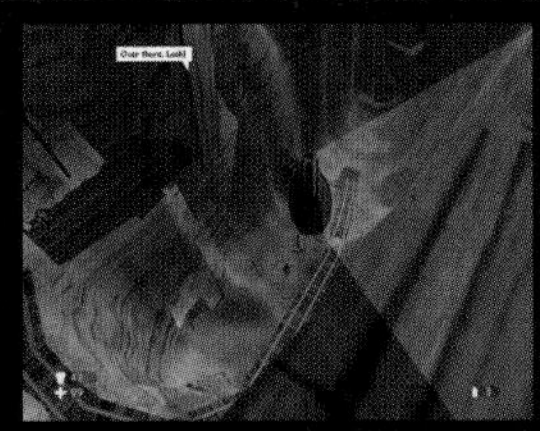

Ride the mining cable down to the platform and pick up the **Bazooka Rockets**, **Full MedKit**, and **Box of BMG50 Ammo**. Walk down the mine cart track to the bottom of the canyon.

As you walk along the canyon floor, you will sense attacks from above. Take out the first thug you sense with long range Bazooka Rockets.

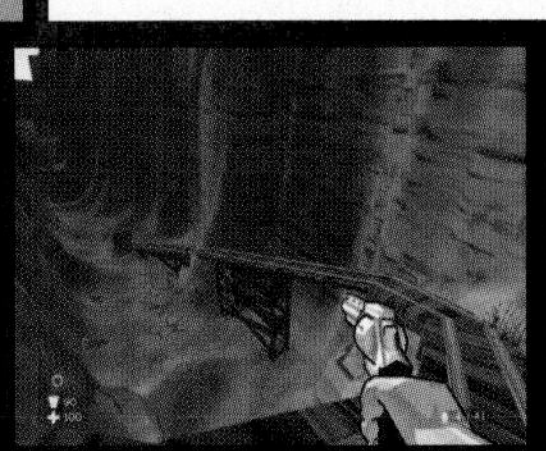

CHECKPOINT: CANYON FLOOR

Keep moving along the canyon floor until you sense another Bazooka attack from above. Send him a bit of the Rocket power that he planned to use on you.

Just past where you kill the second thug you will see a hook in the rocks above. Switch to the Sniper Rifle and look past the hook toward the end of the canyon. Two more thugs are up on a ledge. One of them is armed with a Bazooka. Kill him quickly before he can fire any shots with the Bazooka. Kill the other thug with another shot from the Sniper Rifle.

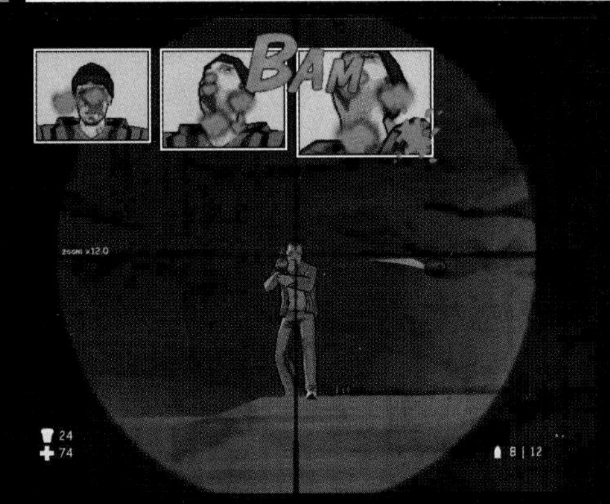

Use the Grappling Hook to pull yourself up to the second ledge on the right-hand side the canyon wall. Switch to the 44 Special, then walk along the cliff edge. Off to the left you will see a break in the cliff pathway and two thugs will attack you. Since they are at such close range, you can use the 44 Special to handle them.

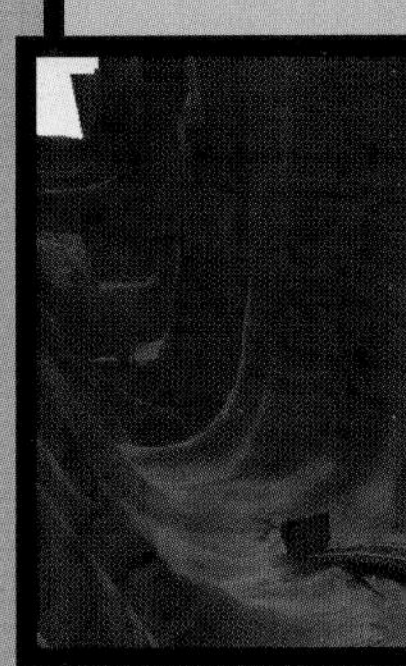

Grab the **Bazooka Rockets** and **Full MedKit** from the cliff path and collect some **Grenades** and **5.56 Ammo** from the dead bodies. You must jump across the opening just ahead.

You move slower with the Bazooka in your hands than with any other weapon. When you try to make a jump, equip a weapon other than the Bazooka or jump with no weapon at all.

Up ahead, one of the thugs is singing. Although he does boast some vocal talent, he is still planning on killing you, XIII. Switch back to the Bazooka and take out two thugs on the ledge across from you, along with the singer on the ledge below.

There are a couple of thugs down on the canyon floor. Drop a **Grenade** down on them. Surprise!

Go back to where you jumped across. From this side, you can make your way down the side of the canyon.

CHECKPOINT: APPROACHING THE RUINS

As you climb down the cliff, stop at the ledge where the singing thug was waiting. Pick up the **Sniper Rifle**, **BMG50 Ammo**, and **Full MedKit** from the far edge of the cliff.

Head back to the area beneath the broken stone bridge, then use the stairstep ledges in the cliff to scale down to the canyon floor.

As you walk along the bottom of the canyon, Jones radios in that there is a way out of the canyons behind the ruins. Switch from the Bazooka to the Kalash, then climb up the two ladders to the top of the canyon.

A single thug patrols the top of the cliff. Thrash him with the Kalash, then turn your attention toward the two **MedKits** and two **Boxes of Cal 12 Ammo** in the side of the ruins.

On the right side of the canyon, a ledge leads up and away from the ruins. Follow it up to where you killed a thug earlier, and grab the **Full MedKit** and two canisters of **Bazooka Rockets**.

You will sense more thugs at the ruins. Switch to the Sniper Rifle and shoot as many as you can from a safe distance.

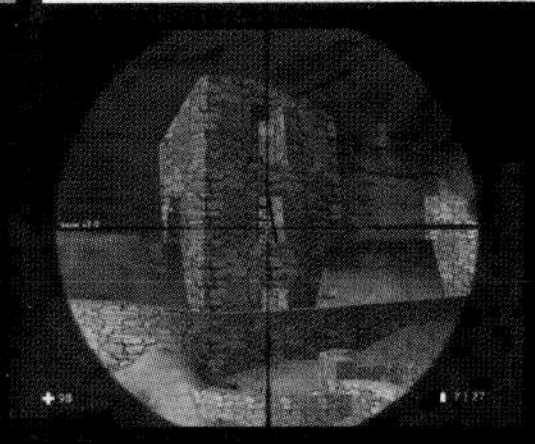

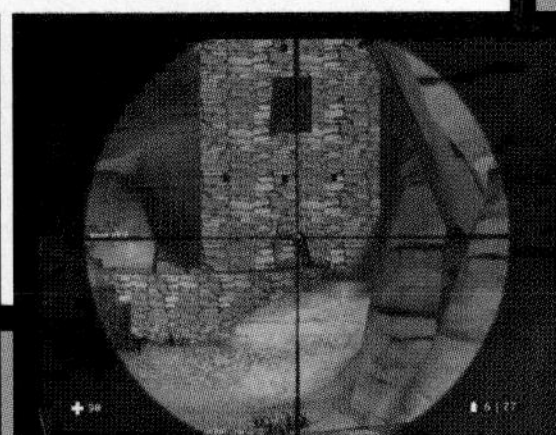

Return to the ruins. As you begin to climb the ladder, you will sense two more thugs. Quickly back down the ladder to avoid a Bazooka attack from the thug on the left. Use the Sniper Rifle to take out both enemies.

Pick up the **MedKit** from the ruins ahead, and walk along the edge of the ruins until you see another **MedKit**. Switch to the Kalash for some close quarters combat. Kill the first thug you see as you walk up the right side of the ruins.

Walk along in front of the buildings. In a building up ahead, you will see a ladder. A thug jumps out and starts shooting. Let him have it with the Kalash, then climb the ladder up to the next level.

A path here leads up the side of the cliff face or around the top of this building to the right. Go around the ruined building to the right on the lower ledge.

Kill the lone thug who pops out of the building up ahead. Then use the Shotgun to shoot away the boards blocking a tunnel entrance in the rear of this structure.

Climb through the entrance and down into the tunnel until it opens up where Jones has hidden the airplane.

Switch over to the Sniper Rifle and climb down to the plane. As you head around to the side of the aircraft, you come under attack from one more thug armed with a Bazooka. Use the Sniper Rifle to find him up on the side of the ruins and take him out.

Approach the plane to finish the mission.

MISSION COMPLETE

Mission 17:
SWIM LIKE A FISH.

MISSION BRIEFING

OBJECTIVES

Infiltrate the SPADS camp.

WEAPONS

9mm
Crossbow
Assault Rifle

ENEMIES

SPADS Soldiers

SUMMARY

Prepare to get wet, XIII. There is a back way into the SPADS camp through some sewage drainage tunnels. Avoid the SPADS patrols and find your way into the base.

QUICK AND DIRTY

Locate the drainage pipe and swim through it. Just as you are about to run out of air, the pipe ends.

Head to the surface for air and wait until the two SPADS soldiers walk out of sight. Use the Hook to pull yourself up on the platform, then throw the switch that opens the second drainage pipe.

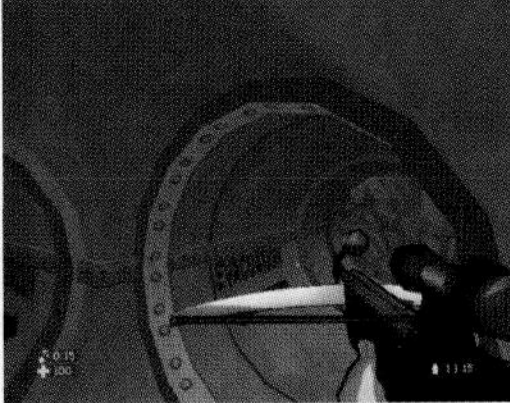

Kill the lone SPADS soldier when he returns, then dive into the water. Swim through the second drainage pipe until you see it branch off to the left. Swim into the left tunnel and surface for air.

Swim back into the drainage pipe until you see a break in the top of the pipe. Enter the tunnel and walk out onto the ledge.

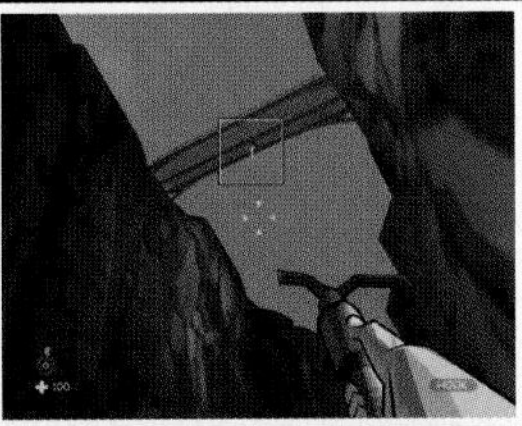

Use the Crossbow to eliminate the two patrolling SPADS soldiers, then use the Hook to swing across to the next ledge. Use the Hook again to swing to a third ledge, then enter the tunnel in the side of the rock.

Climb to the top of the tunnel and listen to the conversation between General Standwell and Colonel MacCall. After they leave, break the grate leading down into the base and climb down the ladder to end the mission.

CHECKPOINT: THE BACK WAY

Swim toward the cliff edge and avoid the searchlight. Dive underwater to locate the drainage tunnel entrance, then head back to the surface for a breath of air before you plunge into the tunnel.

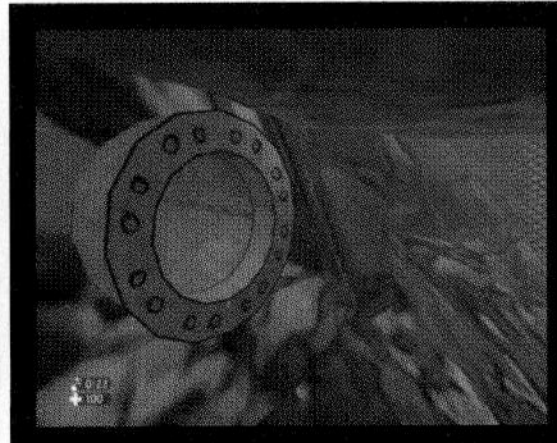

Follow the tunnel along until you see a side passage, then take this route. Right about now you are running out of air, so pop up to the surface and take a breath. Above you two SPADS soldiers are talking about the quality of the new SPADS recruits.

Wait until the soldiers walk away, then use the Hook to pull yourself up onto the platform. Find the switch to open the drainage pipe, and then duck down behind the crates next to the control console.

Switch to the Crossbow and aim right between the crates. A SPADS soldier exits the door at the far end of the walkway and comes very close to where you are hidden. Wait until he turns around and heads back, then plug him in the back of the skull with a Crossbow Bolt.

Grab his Assault Rifle and dive back into the water. Swim through the drainage pipe until you see the pipe branch off to the left, then swim this way and go up for air.

You overhear two SPADS soldiers talking about loading up a submarine. After listening to the conversation, swim back into the drainage pipe. Swim up into the break in the pipe ahead.

This takes you to an underground cave that leads out onto a ledge far below two steel bridges where SPADS soldiers are patrolling.

Switch to the Crossbow and eliminate the SPADS soldiers. Use your Grappling Hook to hang from a hook under the first bridge, then swing over to the next ledge.

From this tiny ledge in the rock, use your Grappling Hook to latch onto another hook under the second bridge, then swing across the chasm to an even smaller ledge. A tunnel there leads into the rock.

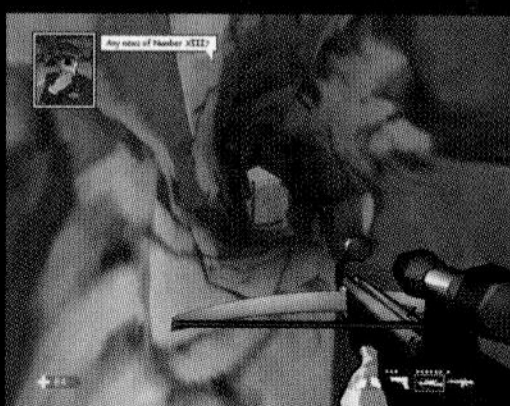

Go through the tunnel, then sneak up to the fence, then stop and listen to the conversation between General Standwell and Colonel MacCall. Don't get too close to the fence or the SPADS soldiers will see you!

After the general and the colonel walk away, head over to the grate and break it, then climb down the ladder. Jones radios in that you have made it inside the base and now need to plant the listening device in Colonel MacCall's tent. Walk forward to end the mission.

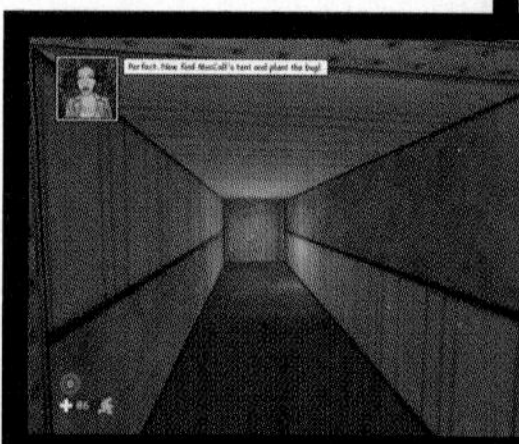

MISSION COMPLETE

Mission 18
SPY VS. SPY.

MISSION BRIEFING

OBJECTIVES

Hide the spy microphone in Colonel MacCall's Tent. Discreetly eliminate the SPADS around the beige tent.

WEAPONS

9mm	Assault Rifle
9mm Silencer	M60
Crossbow	Bomb

ENEMIES

SPADS Soldiers

SUMMARY

Time for stealth, XIII. Find Colonel MacCall's tent and plant a listening device to find out what his plans are. Eliminate the SPADS soldiers guarding his tent, and leave no traces or the secret meeting is off.

QUICK AND DIRTY

Swim through the drainage tunnel and climb up into the shower room. Two soldiers talking will trigger a flashback.

Sneak around and use the Crossbow and Silenced 9mm to kill the five SPADS soldiers in the first compound. Keep them from setting off the alarm. Kill the one SPADS soldier in the warehouse.

Use the Crossbow or Silenced 9mm to kill the three SPADS soldiers in the bamboo field next to a half-finished building. Go down the hallway to another large outdoor SPADS compound.

Take out the tower guard and the searchlight with the Crossbow. Then sneak around behind the crates at the front of the compound and use the Crossbow to eliminate the four SPADS soldiers there.

The alarm must not go off in this last compound or the secret meeting will be called off. Use the Crossbow to kill the tower guard and shoot out the searchlight.

Sneak around and eliminate the remaining three SPADS soldiers protecting Colonel MacCall's tent. As you kill each soldier, grab his body and drag it back to the motor pool so that it's out of sight.

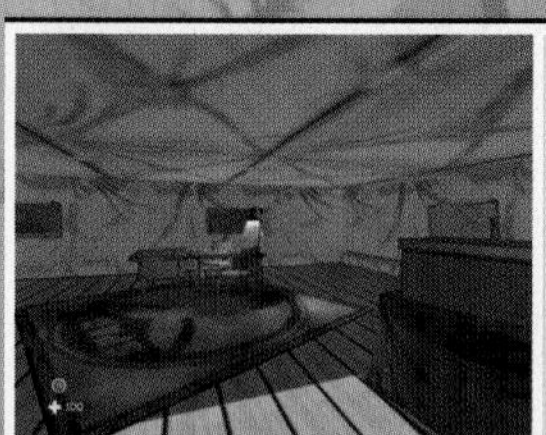

Enter MacCall's tent and plant the listening device, then duck through a small opening and hide out in the back of the tent while Colonel MacCall conducts a secret meeting.

After MacCall leaves, collect the Magnetic Card and the Documents off his desk. Use the Silenced 9mm to kill the two guards waiting outside.

Use the Magnetic Card to open the warehouse. Cross the warehouse and open the door. Use the Crossbow to kill the tower guard, the soldier in the SPADS shack, and a third SPADS soldier out in front of the 'Explosives' building.

Switch to the Assault Rifle and kill the last three SPADS soldiers patrolling the area. Two more are behind the 'Explosives' building.

Use the Lockpick to unlock the red door at the back of the 'Explosives' building. Switch to the Assault Rifle before opening the door, and then kill the solitary soldier inside. Grab the M60, Ammo, and Body Armor, then plant the bomb inside this building.

CHECKPOINT: WHO IS JASON FLY?

Swim down the long drainage tunnel. As you approach the end, you hear two SPADS soldiers talking about a rivalry between Steve Rowland and another SPADS soldier. When you reach the end of the tunnel, swim down to duck under the wall. A ladder leads up into the shower room. Climb it just in time to hear the soldier remember the name of Steve Rowland's rival: Jason Fly. This triggers a flashback.

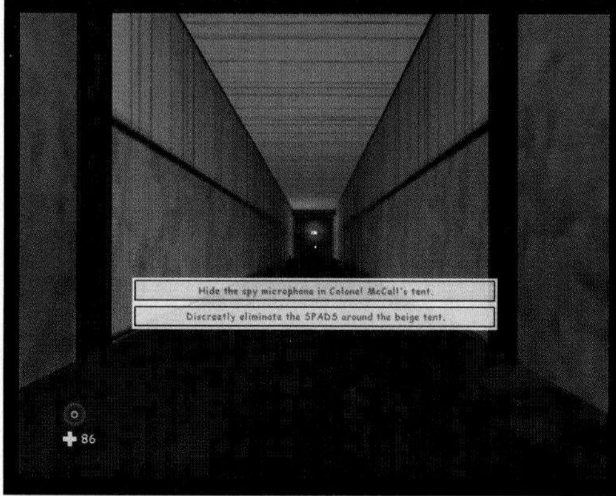

After the flashback, open the shower door and enter the locker room. Pick up the **Important Document**, **9mm Silencer**, and **Crossbow Bolts** from the open lockers.

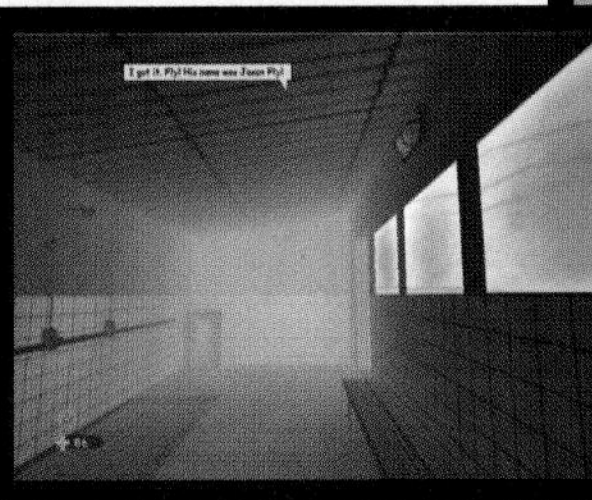

You must use stealth to complete this mission. Switch to the Crossbow, and then open the door. While still in the doorway, target and shoot the SPADS soldier in the guard tower.

While you want to use Stealth for this mission, do not be afraid to use heavy weapons. As long as the SPADS soldiers do not hit the alarm, you can complete the mission. If you trip up and see someone running for an alarm, switch to the Assault Rifle and blow them away before they can trigger the alarm.

Use a second Crossbow Bolt on the searchlight.

Leave the locker room, then head to the right and around the back of the locker building. Look straight ahead, behind the buildings. Wait until a SPADS soldier walks into view, then switch to the Crossbow and plant one right in his forehead.

Switch to the Silenced 9mm and walk to where you just killed the SPADS soldier. Turn around. Wait back here until another SPADS soldier

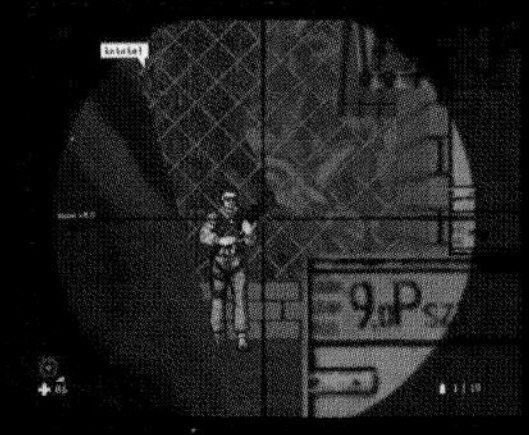

Walk between the two buildings where the SPADS soldier just came from. Across the compound you can see one SPADS soldier on the left patrolling. A second one exits the warehouse. Switch to the Crossbow and kill the soldier leaving the warehouse, then the kill the soldier on the left when he stops to turn around.

That takes care of all the soldiers in this area.

Head over to the guard shack and collect the **MedKit** and the **Important Document**.

Change to the Assault Rifle and open the warehouse door. Inside is a single SPADS soldier. Kill him quickly with a full automatic burst from your weapon.

There are three SPADS soldiers in the next area. Open the door and crouch down. Across from the door are some square vent pipes and some crates, and beyond that is a half-constructed building. Wait until one of the SPADS soldiers goes into the building, then kill him with the Crossbow.

Step out of the door and look to the right. There's another SPADS soldier at the end of the warehouse, next to some round pipes. A Crossbow bolt through the neck should slow him down.

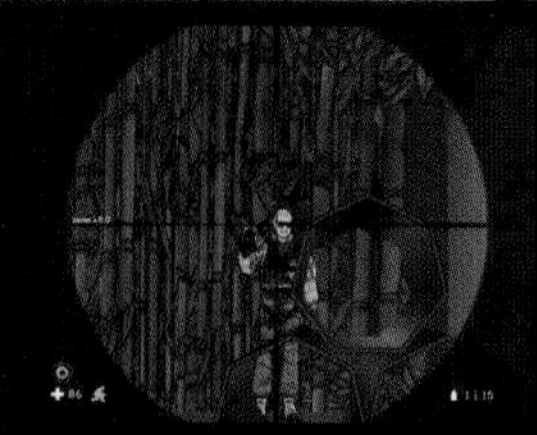

You will see the third soldier start to walk around behind the half-constructed building. Switch to the Silenced 9mm and sneak up behind him. Give him two in the head and one in the chest to put him down for good, then grab the **Box of 9mm Ammo** from the top of a crate behind the construction site. There's a **MedKit** and some **Crossbow Bolts** inside the half-constructed building.

Go through the door in the side of the hill.

CHECKPOINT: HIDE AND SEEK

You need to cross another large SPADS compound. When you open the second door, you hear SPADS soldiers talking. Move off to the left and wait behind the first building until one of the soldiers comes around the corner, then kill him with the Silenced 9mm.

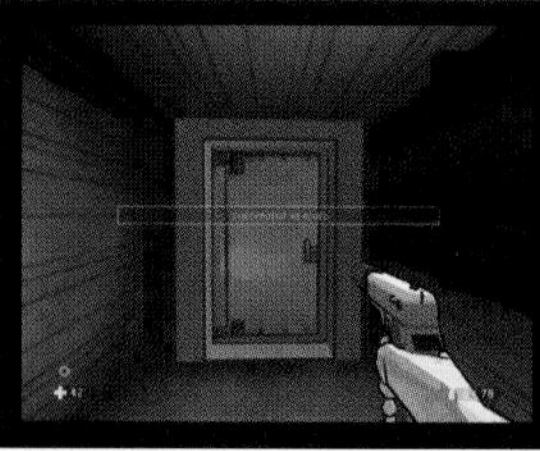

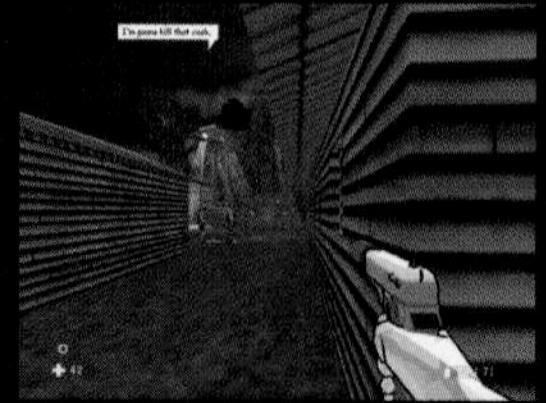

Empty your hands of weapons and grab his body. Drag it behind the building where it is out of sight, and dump it. Go to the back corner of this building and look out across the compound. Use the Crossbow to kill the SPADS soldier in the tower, and shoot out the searchlight.

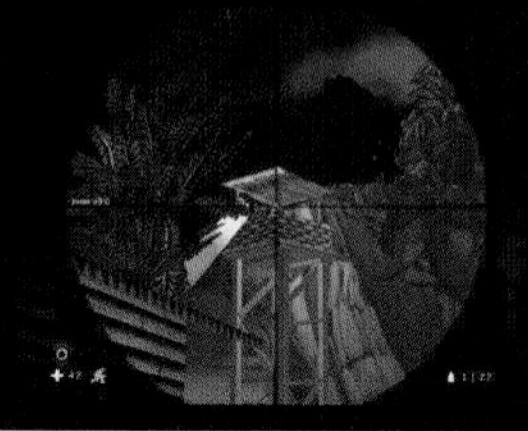

Return to the door you just exited and walk straight across the compound, staying behind the large crates covered with a tarp. You will see a building marked with a Red Cross. Switch to the Silenced 9mm, then go behind the Red Cross building and kill the SPADS soldier you find here.

Return to the boxes and hide behind them. There's another soldier walking around on the far side of the compound, up near another pile of crates and the gate. Switch over to the Crossbow and kill him.

There is one more SPADS soldier left, in the guard shack. Switch back to the Silenced 9mm and walk up behind him. A couple of shots relieves him of his duty.

The large aluminum building on the far side of the compound is a motor pool. Enter it and pick up the **Box of 9mm Ammo** and the **Full MedKit**.

You are near Colonel MacCall's tent, and this is where you need to use the most stealth. Open the back door to the motor pool, then use the Crossbow to spear the SPADS soldier in the guard tower. Shoot out the searchlight with another Bolt.

Move a few feet forward and duck down beside the crates. When the first soldier strolls right in front of your cover, pop up and shoot him with a Crossbow Bolt. It's time for some corpse disposal. Empty your hands of weapons, then carry his body back to the motor pool, and dump it.

Move to the right and crouch down behind the fuel truck. Wait there until a SPADS soldier emerges from behind the tents, then plug him with a Crossbow Bolt. Add his body to the growing stack in the motor pool.

There is one more SPADS soldier waiting in front of Colonel MacCall's tent. Move up near the front of the fuel truck and fire your Crossbow his way, then recover his body and dump it in the motor pool with the others.

Now that the coast is clear, head for Colonel MacCall's tent. Jones gives you instructions on where to place the listening device. After you plant the bug, crouch down and go through the small opening in the side of the tent. Stay in here and out of sight when the Colonel shows up and conducts his secret meeting.

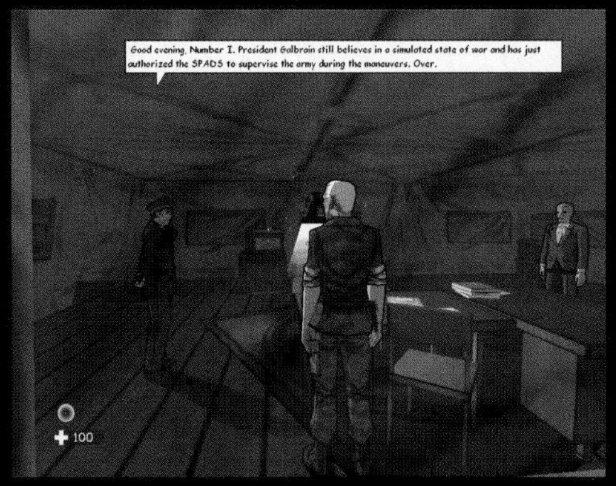

When the meeting ends, duck down through the small tent opening and grab the **Magnetic Card** and the **Document** off MacCall's desk, then backtrack through the small opening and go around to the back of the tent. Pick up the **Full MedKit** off the crates.

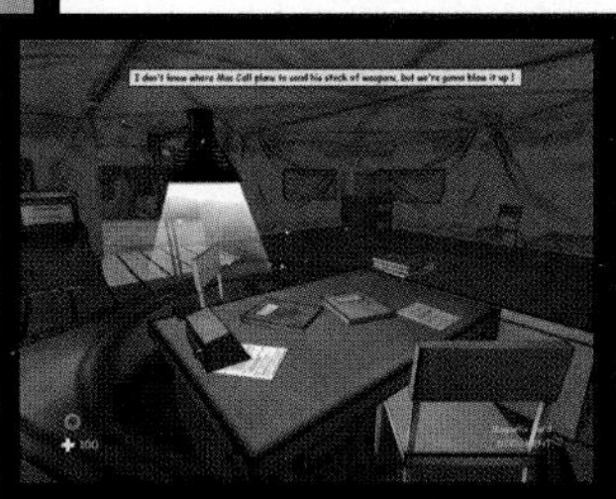

There are two new SPADS soldiers outside the tent. Use the Silenced 9mm to kill them both. Exit through the back of the tent and eliminate the one waiting out back, then do the same to the SPADS soldier in front of the tent.

Use the Magnetic Card to open the warehouse.

CHECKPOINT: BLOW UP THE BASE.

All this sneaking around is getting old, XIII. It's almost time to blow things up! Go through the warehouse and open the door on the other side. You will see three SPADS soldiers talking. Switch to the Crossbow and shoot right over their heads, killing the soldier in the guard tower and shooting out the searchlight.

When one of the SPADS soldiers gets into the guard shack, shoot him with a Crossbow bolt. The guard shack hides his body from the other soldiers.

On the right side of the compound is a large building labeled 'Explosives'. That's where you need to go. Let the other two SPADS soldiers walk away without killing them, then take a few steps forward until you can see a SPADS soldier in front of the Explosives building. Nail him with a Crossbow Bolt and he falls down behind the sandbags where his body is hidden.

With both the tower guard and the soldier in the guard shack dead, you can finally cut loose a little, XIII. Switch to the Assault Rifle. After a few seconds, you will see one of the two soldiers who walked away begin to return. Run across the compound toward the pile of crates.

Jump out from behind the crates and quickly take out two SPADS soldiers with the Assault Rifle, then reload and run around behind the two aluminum shacks. A SPADS soldier is walking away from you. Before he can notice his dead buddies, let him have it with the Assault Rifle.

There's a fuel truck and a Hummer ahead, and you hear two SPADS soldiers talking from around the corner of the building. Make your way past the vehicles, then kill both soldiers with the Assault Rifle.

Use the **Lockpick** on the red door on the side of the large Explosives building. But before you open it, make sure you have the Assault Rifle equipped. Upon entering, a SPADS soldier walks into view. Spray him with bullets.

Pick up the **M60 Machine Gun** and the two **Heavy Helmets** from inside the doorway, then continue past a few generators to open the inside door. This is your destination.

Plant the explosives to end the mission.

MISSION COMPLETE

Mission 19
FROM THE ASHES

MISSION BRIEFING

OBJECTIVES

Escape from the camp!

WEAPONS

9mm
9mm Silencer
Crossbow
Assault Rifle
M60

ENEMIES

SPADS Soldiers
Colonel MacCall

SUMMARY

You survived the explosion, XIII. The SPADS camp is in ruins. Fight your way past the remaining SPADS soldiers and find a way to escape.

QUICK AND DIRTY

After another explosion, run off to the right, then use the mounted machine gun to fight off several waves of SPADS soldiers.

Make your way back across the SPADS compound and the bamboo field, killing any SPADS soldiers you encounter.

Fight Colonel MacCall!

When the colonel is dead, take his Key and exit through the open gate.

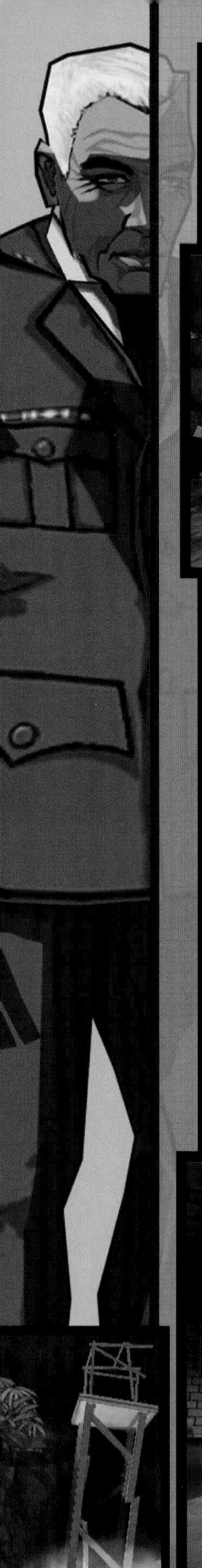

CHECKPOINT: NO SMOKING AREA

After the smoke clears, run off to the right and man the Mounted Machine Gun. Hit Action to arm the weapon, then start shooting at the SPADS soldiers as they storm from the warehouse.

When the SPADS soldier parade ends, abandon the Machine Gun and sprint for the warehouse door. The warehouse is filled with black smoke. Grab a **Full MedKit** off some crates as you exit.

Kill four SPADS soldiers in the compound, then run past MacCall's tent toward the motor pool. Waste the two soldiers you meet there. When three more soldiers run out, shoot an AR Grenade at them to decimate all three in one easy step.

As you cross the motor pool, Jones radios that the SPADS discovered your boat. You must find another way out of the base. Open the warehouse door and enter the large outdoor compound.

CHECKPOINT: MACCALL'S REVENGE

Run across the compound to the door that's set in the tunnel. You overhear a SPADS soldier talking to Colonel MacCall. When Sgt. Bauer steps out, pour a clip from the Assault Rifle into him.

Enter the bamboo field and kill off the two soldiers still guarding this area, then cross the warehouse and open the door leading to the first compound.

Upon entering, Colonel MacCall makes you an offer you can easily refuse. When he's done talking, the fight is on!

BOSS FIGHT: COLONEL MACCALL

Armed with the Assault Rifle, AR Grenades, M60 machine gun, and regular Grenades, the fight against Colonel MacCall is pretty easy.

Soften him up at long range with a couple of AR Grenades, then switch to the M60 to finish him off!

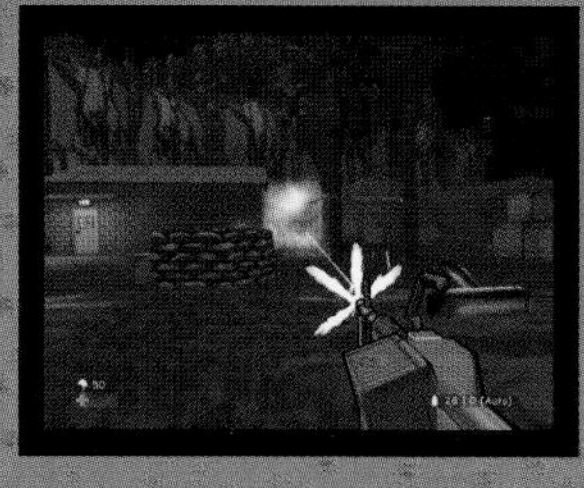

When the Colonel is dead, pick up some Grenades, M60 Ammo, and a Key from his body. Exit through the open gate and use the Key on the side door to complete the mission.

MISSION COMPLETE

Mission 20:
PATRIOT GAMES

MISSION BRIEFING

OBJECTIVES

Infiltrate the submarine before it leaves.

WEAPONS

9mm	Assault Rifle
9mm Silencer	M60
Crossbow	Grenades

ENEMIES

Dock Workers
SPADS soldiers

SUMMARY

With your boat in the hands of the SPADS, you must find another way to escape, XIII. Fight or Sneak your way past the SPADS soldiers and Dock Workers, then infiltrate the USS Patriot submarine before it sets sail.

QUICK AND DIRTY

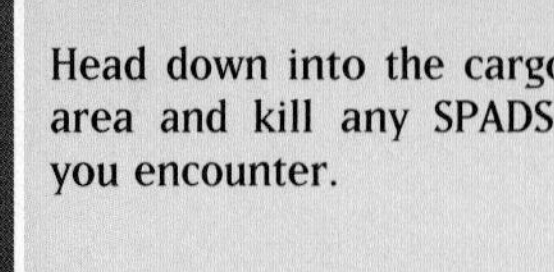

Head down into the cargo loading area and kill any SPADS soldiers you encounter.

Pick up some extra Ammo and Body Armor in a side room, then take out a group of SPADS soldiers as they march by.

The large doors are starting to close. Run through three doors and into a long hallway where you can see several vehicles.

Kill the Dock Workers and SPADS soldiers, then enter the watertight door and head up into the cargo loading control center. Eliminate the SPADS soldiers there.

Skewer the four SPADS patrolling the cargo loading bay with your Crossbow, then use the Grappling Hook to lower yourself to the floor.

Climb two ladders on the right side of the room to a ledge high above the cargo bay floor, then enter the vent.

Lower yourself down the vent and onto the submarine platform. Kill all the SPADS soldiers and Dock Workers guarding the submarine.

Climb the ladder on the side of the submarine and enter the sub through the open hatch.

CHECKPOINT: SUBMARINE RACES

Enter the red watertight door and descend the stairs. You will hear a couple of SPADS soldiers talking. Equip the M60 machine gun and kill them.

Near the bottom of the stairs you encounter another pair of SPADS soldiers. Waste them. Scour the room off to the side to find **Crossbow Bolts**, a **MedKit**, a **Heavy Helmet**, and a **Heavy Vest**.

Open the next red watertight door. Down a short hallway you can see four SPADS soldiers in Heavy Vests and Heavy Helmets marching by. Equip a Grenade and wait until they walk past. Burn off about one minute of time on the Grenade, and then drop it right into the middle of the group.

The large security doors are beginning to close. Duck under the closest door. Equip the Assault Rifle, and then make a run for the next door. Keep running down the hallways and through the next large security door before it shuts.

CHECKPOINT: CARGO LOADING CENTER

This large hallway houses vehicles and a couple of Dock Workers lounging near some crates. Off to the right of the doorway, next to some crates, you can grab two **Assault Rifles**, **AR Grenades,** and **AR Ammo**.

Use an AR Grenade to blast the leisurely Dock Workers, then switch to the M60. Four SPADS soldiers in heavy gear rush from a watertight door at the end of the hallway. Take cover behind the vehicles or crates, then pick them off with the M60.

Collect **Grenades**, **AR Ammo** and **Light Vests** from the dead Soldiers, then enter the watertight door and go up the stairway. Kill the two SPADS soldiers in the control room.

From there, go onto a platform high above a large loading area. You can see four SPADS soldiers patrolling below. Switch to the Crossbow and spear all four of them from your perch.

Time for some trick acrobatics, XIII. At the end of the platform, you can see two places to connect your Grappling Hook. Latch onto the hook closer to the ceiling, then pull yourself up on top of some girders. Swing over to the girders, then quickly release your Grappling Hook.

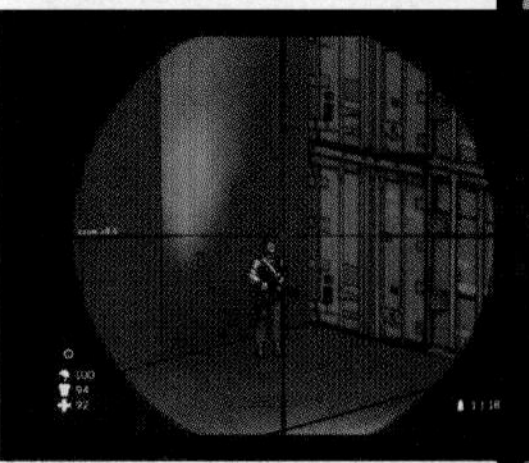

Approach the edge of the girder assembly so you can see another place to attach your Hook.

Hook up again, and then swing over onto the top of the highest red cargo container on the left. It's a bit of a jump. As soon as you connect your Hook, reel yourself in enough to get swinging. Then release the Hook and land on top of the cargo container.

Drop off the edge to find a **Full MedKit**, **AR Grenades**, **Crossbow Bolts**, and **Boxes of AR Ammo**.

Jump across the small gap and onto the next cargo container. Directly above the end of the container you can see another place to connect your Grappling Hook. Pull yourself up and swing over to some pipes.

Walk along the pipes to the vent grate in the corner, then break it open and crawl into the vent. There's a sheer drop at the end of this line, but there's another place to connect the Grappling Hook above you. Do so, then gradually lower yourself.

Below, a SPADS Soldier is keeping guard. Wait until he moves out of sight, then lower yourself all the way to the floor.

Equip the M60 and eliminate all the SPADS soldiers and Dock Workers on the platform around the submarine.

The submarine is getting ready to set sail, XIII. You have just enough time to get aboard. Run down the right side of the platform and onto the rocks. Near the rear of the submarine you can see an open hatch. Dive into the water and climb up the ladder on the side of the sub.

Then climb down into the open hatch to end the mission.

MISSION COMPLETE

Mission 21:
SUBMARINE HIDE AND SEEK

MISSION BRIEFING

OBJECTIVES

Find the radio and contact Jones. Hide in the officer's cabin. Avoid being spotted and don't kill the captain.

WEAPONS

9mm	Assault Rifle
9mm Silencer	AR Grenades
Crossbow	Grenades

ENEMIES

Submarine Crew

SUMMARY

Welcome aboard the USS Patriot, XIII. Find a radio and let Jones know your location, then hide out in the Officer's Cabin until the submarine reaches its destination. Stealth is a priority; do not let anyone see you!

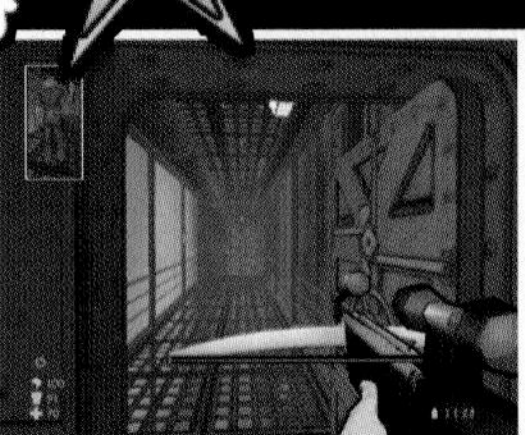

Exit the door and climb down the first ladder. Sneak past the guards to avoid setting off any alarms.

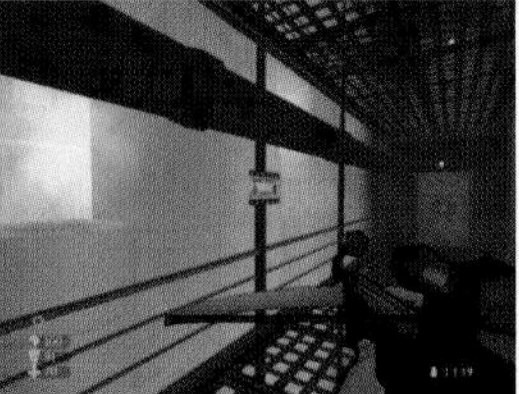

Wait in the small hallway until the captain leaves, then open the inner door and go around to the other one. Eliminate any crewmembers who get in your way with the Crossbow.

Climb back to the upper level and make your way to the radio room. Listen to the captain's conversation, then radio your position to Jones.

Find the crew quarters and hide in the shower of the officer's cabin.

CHECKPOINT: DIVE! DIVE! DIVE!

Exit the door to the left, XIII, then descend the ladder. You will sense trouble. Arm your Crossbow and look down the ladder to the next level. Sure enough, a crewmember is standing at the base of the ladder armed with an Assault Rifle. Let him have a Crossbow Bolt through the top of the head.

Locked doors in the submarine cannot be opened with your Lockpick, XIII. Obtain a Key or find a different door.

When you sense that the crewmember on the level above has walked away and is at the far end of the walkway, open the door. Look across to the left where you can see another crewmember on an upper walkway. Go ahead and shoot him with a Crossbow Bolt. The pipes and equipment keep the crewmember directly above you from seeing him die.

Head down the walkway and through the next watertight door, then close it behind you. You are in a short hallway in front of another watertight door. Before you open it, you will sense a crewmember walking away. Continue to wait. After another few seconds, you will sense the Submarine Captain walking overhead. Wait until he leaves the area before opening the door.

Open the door, then head down the hallway and around to the left. Both doors at the end of the hallway are locked. Use the Crossbow to kill the submarine crewmember up ahead.

Enter the open door at the end of the hallway, then go through the next one to reach the platform. The body of the first crewmember you killed is on the platform above you. Time for a little déjà vu. Look at the upper platform on the left, and then use the Crossbow to kill the patrolling crewmember when he comes into view.

Open the door at the end of the walkway and climb the ladder to the next level. Since you eliminated both the guards on this upper level, you are safe here. Open the door at the end of the walkway.

Pass through the next room and open the door on the left. There is a crewmember patrolling up here. Wait in the doorway until he walks into view, then pierce him with the Crossbow.

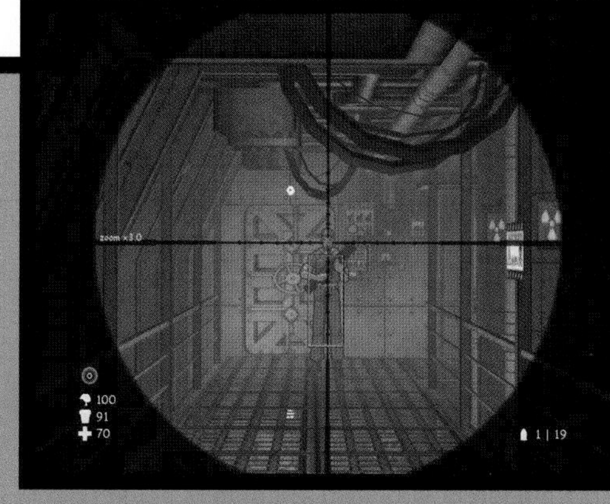

Open the door straight ahead. Inside you will see the Captain working at a control console. When you step into the room you will see him radio the submarine's position to one of the conspirators. This triggers a flashback.

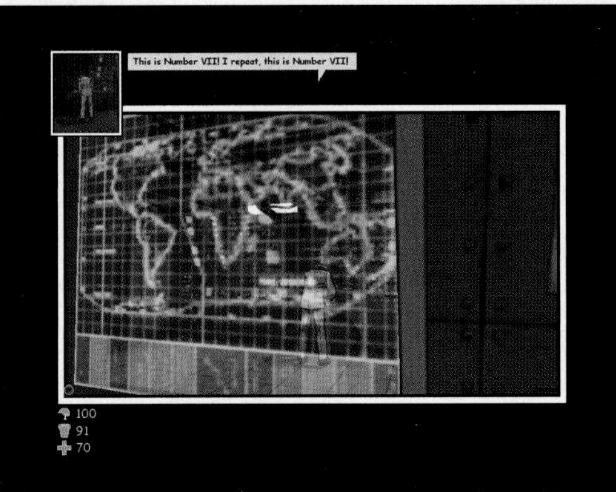

Following the flashback, descend the stairs to listen in on Number I's conversation.

With the Captain gone, you are clear to use the radio to contact Jones.

CHECKPOINT: OFFICER'S QUARTERS

Enter the door on the other side of the radio room, then continue through the left side door in the next room.

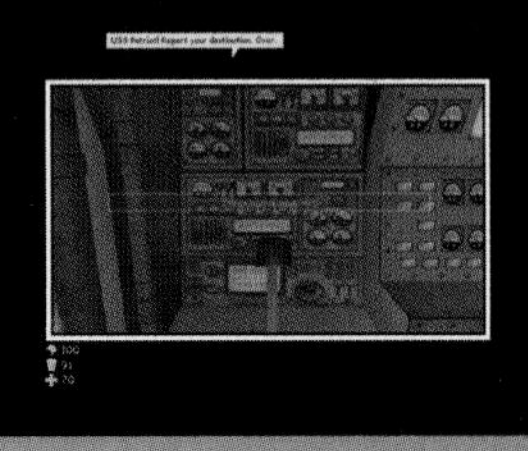

This is the crew quarters. A single crewmember is patrolling this area. Zap him with a Crossbow Bolt, then empty your hands of weapons and pick up the body. Dump the corpse in the officer's cabin, and then hide in the shower to end the mission.

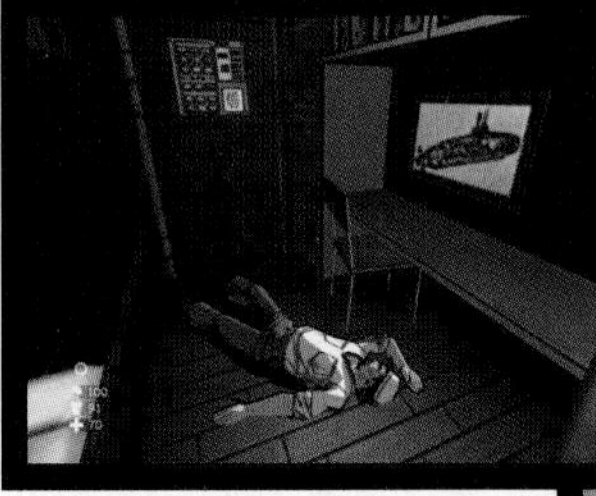

MISSION COMPLETE

Mission 22:
TORPEDO AWAY!

MISSION BRIEFING

OBJECTIVES

You've been spotted! Escape through the torpedo airlock. Find the torpedo lock key.

WEAPON

Assault Rifle

ENEMIES

Submarine Crew
Captain Pacha

SUMMARY

You should have chosen a better hiding spot, XIII. You've been discovered! Time to make a daring escape. Fight your way past the USS Patriot's crew and escape the sub through a torpedo tube.

QUICK AND DIRTY

Crud! You've been discovered! Kill the USS Patriot crewmember who finds you, then load up with weapons and ammo from the Ammo locker.

Fight your way through the submarine to the ladders leading down into the lower deck. Descend both ladders to the lowest level.

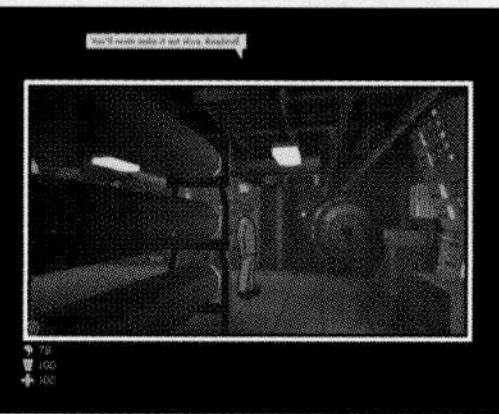

Fight your way through the sub until you are in the torpedo room. Fight Captain Pacha!

Take Captain Pacha's Key and climb up to the control/navigation center. Kill all the crewmembers in there.

Grab the Harpoon Gun and Torpedo Room Key from the captain's cabin, then climb back down into the torpedo room and open the torpedo launcher door with the Key.

Fight the last two crewmembers while you wait for the torpedo bay door to open. Enter the torpedo tube to end the mission.

CHECKPOINT: CAUGHT IN THE ACT

A passing crewmember discovers you in your hiding spot. As he runs away, kill him with the Assault Rifle, XIII.

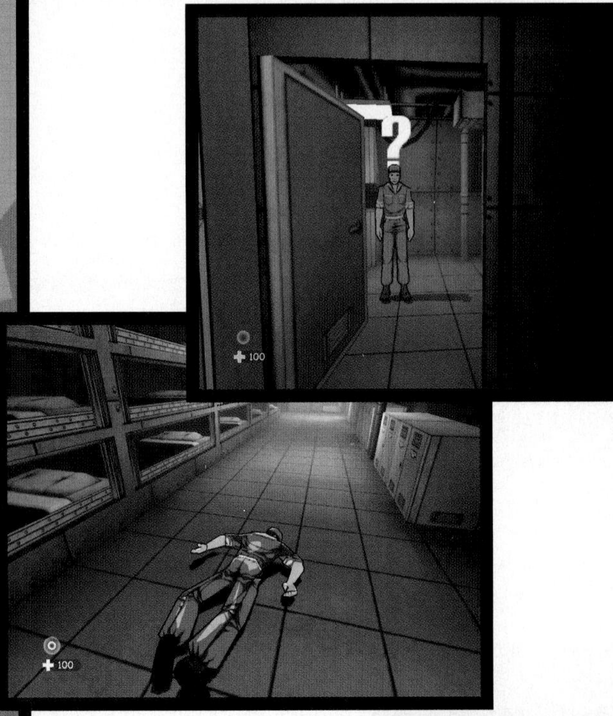
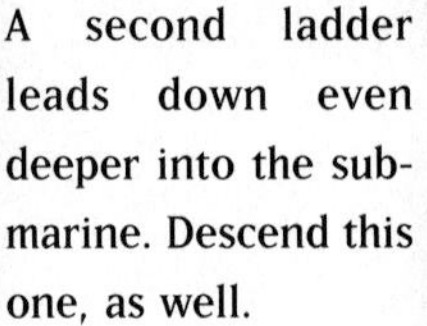

A glass case at the end of the hallway contains a dozen **Assault Rifles**. Smash the glass and take the rifles for extra **AR Ammo**, then pick up the **Heavy Helmet**, **Heavy Vest**, and **MedKit**.

Now that you're armed to the hilt, fight your way back through the sub! Collect more **AR Ammo** from the dead crewmembers and keep an eye out for **MedKits**.

When you reach the ladder to the lower level, climb down. Watch out for the crewmember at the bottom.

A second ladder leads down even deeper into the submarine. Descend this one, as well.

CHECKPOINT: YOUR SHIP'S CAPTAIN

You are in unfamiliar territory, XIII. Watch your back as you fight your way down several hallways. Crewmembers come up from behind you and out both doors in every room. Keep blasting away at them with the Assault Rifle.

Help yourself to the **Full MedKit** and **Heavy Vest** in the galley. Once you kill the two crewmembers in there, make sure you are healed back to full strength, and then reload your weapon.

Watch out for the crewmembers in the dining hall. Two of them will overturn a table and use it for cover.

Next comes the torpedo room where you will fight Captain Pacha!

BOSS FIGHT: CAPTAIN PACHA

Compared to Colonel MacCall and Doctor Johansson, Captain Pacha is a wimp. He is armed with only a MiniGun.

Use the torpedo racks as cover while you hammer away at him with the Assault Rifle.

Two crewmembers armed with 9mm handguns will join the fight. Eliminate them, and then finish off the captain.

When Captain Pacha is dead, collect his MiniGun and his Key. Use the Key to open the hatch in the ladder leading up. You must find the Torpedo Room Key to open the torpedo tubes and escape.

Climb the ladder and enter the control/navigation room. Kill the crewmembers piloting the submarine.

The door on the right side of the room leads to the captain's cabin. Collect the **Torpedo Lock Key** and **Harpoon Gun** inside.

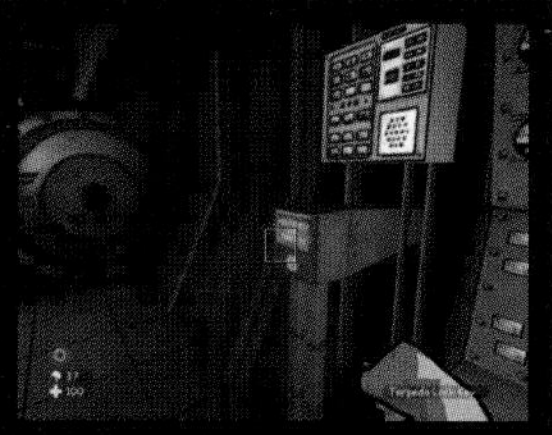

Exit the Control/Navigation room and climb back down into the torpedo room. Use the Torpedo Lock Key on the control panel.

Two more crewmembers attack while you are waiting for the torpedo tube door to open. Eliminate them, then enter the torpedo tube to end the mission.

MISSION COMPLETE

Mission 23:

SUBMARINE SABOTAGE

MISSION BRIEFING

OBJECTIVES

Open the floodgates and leave the hangar.
Sabotage the submarine's propeller.

WEAPONS

- 9mm
- Crossbow
- Assault Rifle
- Harpoon Gun
- Grenades

ENEMIES

- SPADS Soldiers
- Army Soldiers
- Navy Frogmen

SUMMARY

Complete your escape from the USS Patriot submarine by opening the underwater floodgate and swimming to safety. Give them a little going away present, XIII. Sabotage the USS Patriot's propeller before you leave.

Climb out of the water and onto the dock. Eliminate any SPADS and Army soldiers there, then collect Ammo and MedKits from the top of some cargo crates.

Move along the dock next to the submarine until you come to another cargo loading area. Eliminate any SPADS and Army soldiers you encounter.

Climb up the ladder to the second floor platform, then ascend another ladder to the third floor platform.

Throw the Generator switch, then use the Crossbow to take out some snipers from above the control room.

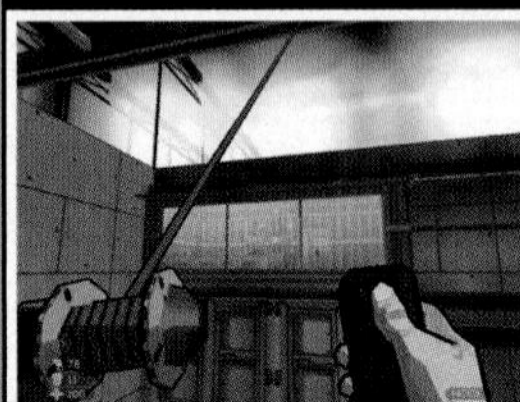

Jump onto the torpedo platform and ride it over the submarine until you see a hook. Use the Grappling Hook to swing over to the control room.

Hit the floodgate switch, then dive into the water below. Plant the bomb on the submarine's propeller and take cover.

Equip the Harpoon Gun and dive into the water, then swim along side the submarine using the Harpoon Gun to eliminate the Navy frogmen.

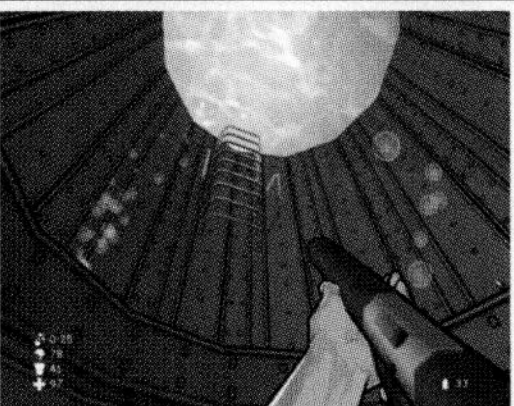

Swim into the left floodgate tunnel and continue left until you see an exit leading up. Climb the ladder to finish the mission.

CHECKPOINT: FIGHT ON THE DOCK

You've successfully fled the submarine, XIII. Complete your escape by opening the floodgates and swimming to safety. When you drop into the water, swim along the floodgate wall toward the edge of the dock. You can see a ladder leading up out of the water.

A lone SPADS soldier is patrolling near these cargo crates. Kill him with the Assault Rifle. As soon as he's dead, an Army soldier comes out of a doorway on the upper platform and a second SPADS soldier begins shooting at you from behind some crates. Another Army soldier emerges from a side door.

In the far corner of the room you can see a ladder leading to the upper platform. Make your away around the boxes and crates. A SPADS soldier is waiting at the bottom of the ladder.

Climb up the ladder to the platform. You can see that there are **AR Grenades**, a **MedKit**, **Harpoon Gun**, and **Grenades** on top of the crates. Jump from crate to crate and collect these items.

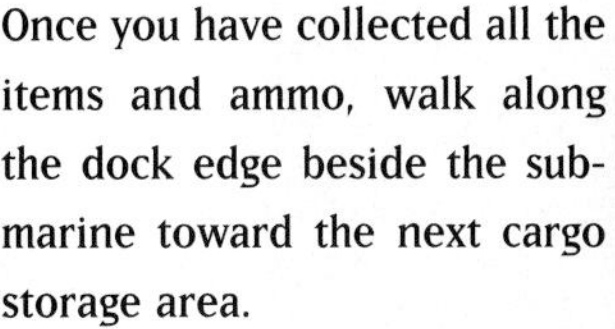

Once you have collected all the items and ammo, walk along the dock edge beside the submarine toward the next cargo storage area.

Some Grenades are right in front of you on a crate marked 'US Army.' To the right, behind some crates, is an Army soldier. Keep moving around to the right where there is a SPADS soldier hiding. Behind him, you'll find a **Full MedKit** and four **Grenades** on a crate.

Head back around the crates to the bay door that leads to the next cargo area. You will sense three soldiers about to attack, two SPADS and one Army. Pick up the three **Grenades** on the Army crate, then move up to the open cargo bay door. There is a crate here with four more **Grenades**.

You can make short work of these soldiers using **AR Grenades**. Launch one at each of the three, aiming just above and behind them. The explosions will obliterate the bunch.

Next, you will sense two more SPADS soldiers coming to attack. One of them is on the platform above you, and the other comes out of a side door on your level. Use the Assault Rifle to eliminate these two enemies.

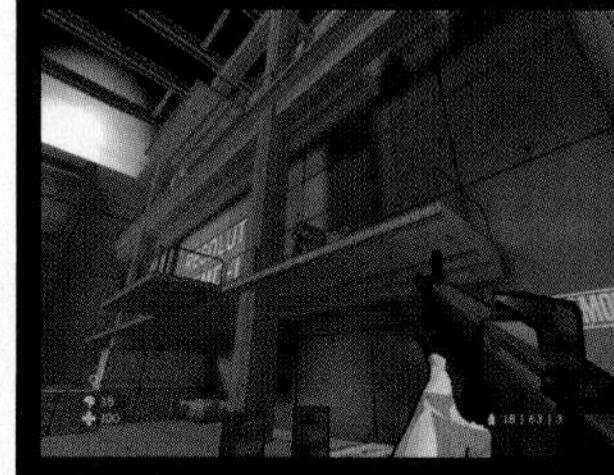

Grab the **AR Ammo** from the bodies and collect a **Crossbow** from behind some crates.

Climb up the ladder at the end of the dock. Behind an open door where one of the SPADS soldiers exited, you can find a **MedKit** and a **Crossbow**.

Another ladder leads to the third floor platform. Climb up and kill the SPADS soldier at the top.

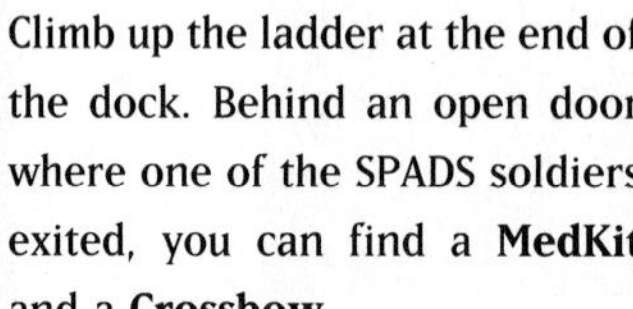

Throw the switch on the Generator to start moving the torpedo loading platform. Quickly duck behind a steel girder, three soldiers will start firing on you from above a control room. Change to the **Crossbow** and eliminate all three soldiers.

Jump over onto the torpedo-loading platform. Shoot out the windows of the control room, then equip the Grappling Hook and swing off the torpedo platform and into the control room.

Grab the **Full MedKit** and **Heavy Vest** out of the back room, then collect the **Harpoon Gun** and **Harpoons** off the side of the control console. Hit the Hydraulic Gate switch to open the floodgates.

CHECKPOINT: SWIMMING WITH SHARKS

Jones radios that you need to sabotage the submarine's propeller. Jump right out the control room window and dive into the water below.

Swim over to the submarine propeller and plant the bomb, then get the heck out of there! Use the ladder to climb up onto the dock and duck down behind some crates until the bomb explodes.

Grab the **MedKit**, **Harpoon Gun**, and **Harpoons** from the crates. Equip the Harpoon Gun, then dive back into the water.

Navy frogmen attack you below the surface. Shoot them with the Harpoon Gun as you swim along the side of the submarine to the floodgate. When you return to the surface for air, watch out for the SPADS soldiers on the dock.

Swim into the floodgate on the left and down the left-hand tunnel until you see an opening leading up. Climb up the ladder to complete the mission.

MISSION COMPLETE

Mission 24:
DEATH FROM ABOVE

MISSION BRIEFING

OBJECTIVES

Find Carrington on quay 33.

WEAPONS

- 9mm
- 44 Special
- Crossbow
- Assault Rifle
- Bazooka
- AR Grenades
- Grenades

ENEMIES

- SPADS Soldiers
- Attack Helicopter

SUMMARY

You're almost home free, XIII. Meet with General Carrington and Colonel Amos on the docks at quay 33 and turn over the file on Steve Rowland. The Army and SPADS soldiers will try to stop you. Find a way through the cargo loading warehouses.

QUICK AND DIRTY

Climb the crates and jump through a window into the warehouse. Head down the ladder and along the walkway to the control room. Drop a cargo container on two unsuspecting soldiers.

Climb down the ladder to the warehouse floor and eliminate any SPADS and Army soldiers in there.

When the truck arrives and the warehouse door, fight the soldiers guarding the vehicle.

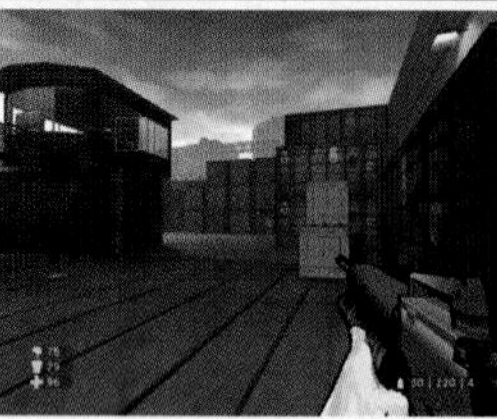

Exit the warehouse and head for the dock. Kill the soldier in the overhead control room and the two soldiers guarding the control tower.

Throw the switch in the control tower to smash a cargo container into the warehouse wall. Climb some crates and jump through the smashed wall.

Kill all the soldiers in the warehouse, then grab the Bazooka and the File on XIII from the radio room. Find the Magnetic Card and exit the warehouse.

Destroy the Attack Chopper with Bazooka Rockets!

Meet with General Carrington and Colonel Amos at the end of the dock to complete the mission.

CHECKPOINT: WHO'S IN CHARGE OF THESE CRATES?

Climb up the crates and jump through the window into the warehouse. Down below you can overhear an Army solider talking to a SPADS sergeant. While they're busy, climb down the ladder and grab the **Box of AR Ammo**, **Box of M60 Ammo**, and two **MedKits**.

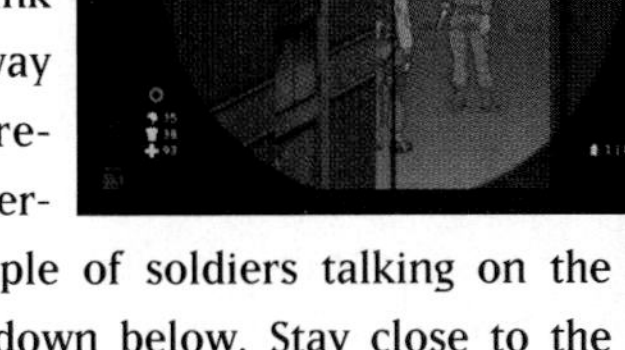

While the soldiers are still talking, exit the door and slink along the walkway beside the warehouse. You will overhear another couple of soldiers talking on the warehouse floor down below. Stay close to the wall so they don't spot you.

Enter the control room. Are those soldiers standing right under that cargo crate? Pull the release lever and send it smashing down on top of them. Ouch!

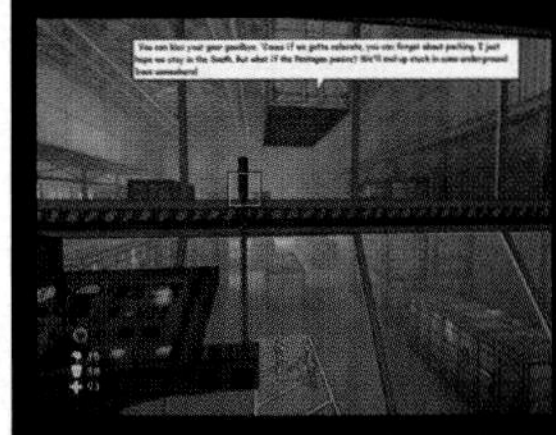

Attracted by the noise, two SPADS soldiers and one Army soldier come running. Exit the control room's side door and grab the **Crossbow Bolts**. Duck down behind the crates and equip the Crossbow. Take out the first SPADS soldier with a Crossbow Bolt. When the second SPADS soldier starts shooting at you from below, pop up from behind the boxes and hit him with a Bolt of his own. Use the Assault Rifle to kill the Army soldier.

Switch to the Grappling Hook and latch onto the hook above you. Then swing onto the top of the cargo container dead ahead.

Turn to the left and hang from the next hook, then swing again, this time onto the top of either of the two cargo containers in front of you.

Equip the Assault Rifle and kill the SPADS soldier below before you try to make it across to the next container.

Use the hook above to swing over to the next container, then jump across to the container directly under the last hook.

You can see a cargo container hanging from a ceiling assembly. There's a **Bazooka**, **Bazooka Rockets**, and **MedKit** on top of the container. Swing over there and claim your prizes.

Use the last hook to lower yourself to the warehouse floor, then enter the radio room and collect the **AR Grenades**, **Assault Rifle**, and **MedKit**. Grab the **Box of 44 Ammo**, **Box of AR Ammo**, **Light Helmet**, and **Light Vest** from the cage.

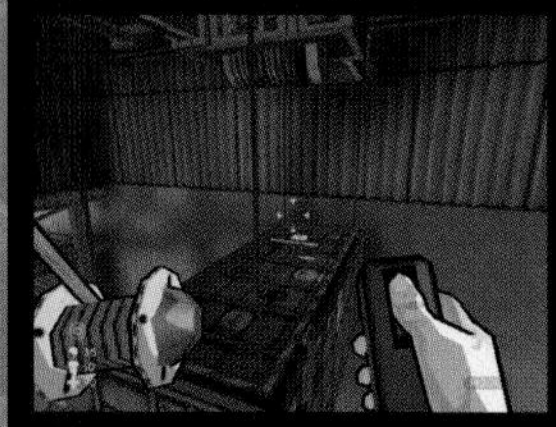

There's also a **Box of M60 Ammo** on a crate under the walkway. A truck arrives and the warehouse door opens. Kill the Army soldier and the two SPADS soldiers, then exit the warehouse.

Use the Crossbow to puncture the SPADS soldier in the control room on the right. Grab the four **Grenades** off the crate and kill the two SPADS soldiers guarding the control room. Search around behind the cargo containers to find **AR Grenades**, **Grenades**, and a **MedKit**.

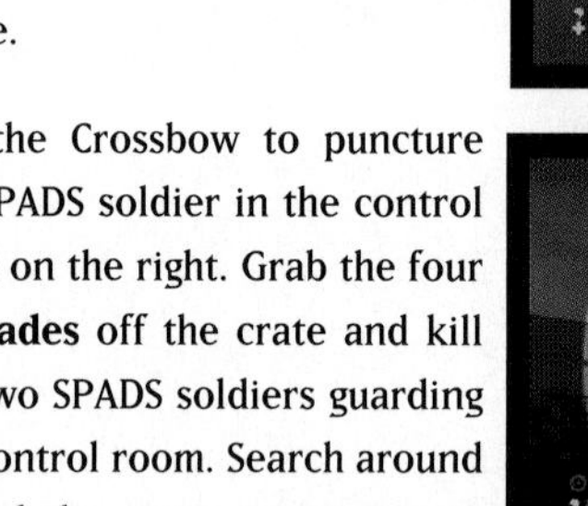

Climb the ladder into the control room. Grab the two **MedKits** and **M60** machine gun. Throw the switch on the control panel to send a cargo container smashing into the warehouse wall.

When the smoke clears, you can climb the crates and jump through the hole in the wall.

Go through the door and out into the warehouse. Equip the M60 machine gun and kill the Army and SPADS soldiers that greet you.

The SPADS have called in an Attack Chopper. Grab the **Box of M60 Ammo** and **Box of AR Ammo** from outside the radio room, then go inside and pick up the **Bazooka**. In one of the cabinets you can also obtain the **File on XIII**, **Bazooka Rockets**, and a **MedKit**.

Even more **Bazooka Rockets** and a **Full MedKit are stashed** in the cage outside the radio room.

Climb the ladder next to the Attack Chopper and enter the office at the end of the platform, then get the **Magnetic Card** and **Full MedKit** in there. Climb the ladder and grab a **Heavy Helmet** and **Light Vest**.

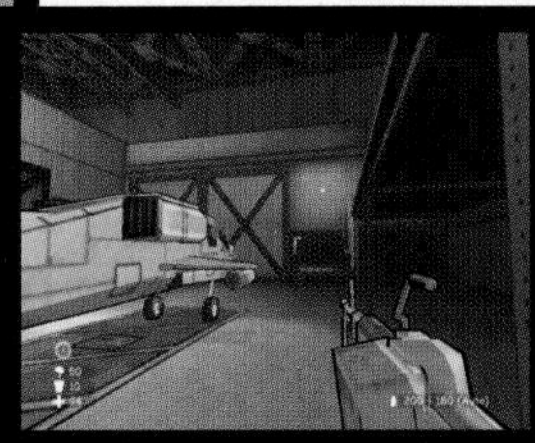

Use the **Magnetic Card** to open the side door. As soon as the door opens, the Attack Chopper arrives. Use the Bazooka to blast it from sky!

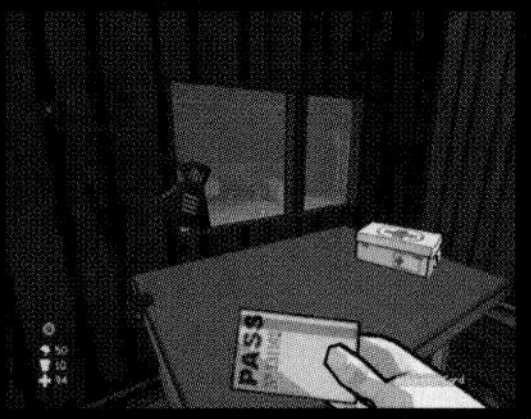

BOSS FIGHT: ATTACK CHOPPER

The Attack Chopper attacks you with rockets and a high-powered machine gun. Take cover behind the tall crates as soon as you exit the warehouse.

You are safe behind the tall cargo container. Pop out from the sides of the container and shoot Bazooka Rockets at the Attack Chopper. As soon as you have fired a rocket, duck back down.

Aim right for the center of the Chopper. It will dodge around a little. When it stops moving and fires a rocket in your direction, return a Bazooka rocket back at it.

Take cover when the Attack Chopper is using the machine gun. It launches two rockets between machine gun bursts.

When you run out of rockets, search the dock for more, then immediately return to the safety of the cargo container.

Eight rockets should bring down the Chopper. Make each shot count!

CHECKPOINT: CHOPPER ATTACK.

The destroyed Attack Chopper will spiral out of control and smash into the dock.

Head down the docks past the wreckage and meet with General Carrington and Colonel Amos to complete the mission.

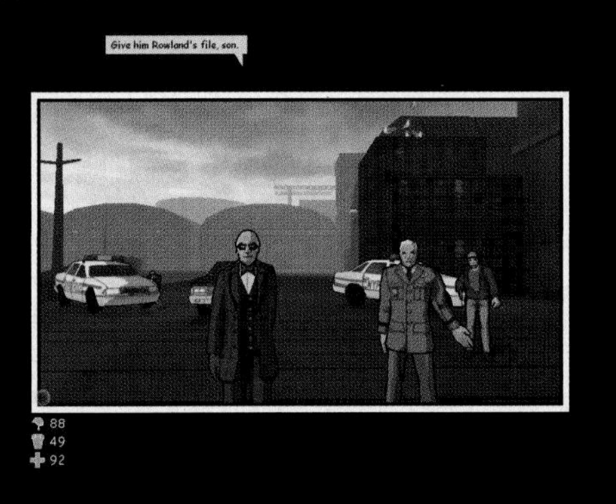

Mission 25:
SECRET MEETINGS

MISSION BRIEFING

OBJECTIVES

Eliminate the guards without raising the alarm. Spy on the meeting from room 41 and record the conversation. Willard and Winslow must not be allowed to escape. Cut the power to the elevators! Help the FBI Agents. Eliminate Winslow. Eliminate Willard.

WEAPONS

- 9mm
- 9mm Silencer
- 44 Special
- Shotgun
- MiniGun
- Dual MiniGun
- Assault Rifle

ENEMIES

- SPADS Soldiers
- Number IX - Winslow
- Number V - Willard

SUMMARY

Time to go back to work for the good guys, XIII. Colonel Amos has assigned you the task of spying on a secret meeting. Discreetly eliminate the guards, then find Room 41 and use the Shotgun mike to record the conversation.

QUICK AND DIRTY

Discreetly eliminate any guards you find patrolling the hotel hallways. Hide the bodies.

Get the key to Room 41 out of the cloakroom. Eliminate the guard in Room 42, then hide his body.

When the Mongoose and Willard arrive, record the conversation.

Shut off the power to the elevator, then assist the FBI Agents.

Climb up the elevator shaft and into the room above the billiard room. Shoot out the glass ceiling, then eliminate Winslow.

Grab Winslow's documents and Key, then open the billiard room door.

Prevent Willard from escaping. Trap him in the meeting room and kill him.

CHECKPOINT: HOTEL SECURITY

Exit the elevator. The first room on the right is a hotel linen closet. Go up to the corner and wait until the female guard walks by. Sneak up behind her and knock her unconscious. Grab the body and dump it in the hotel linen closet, then collect her **MiniGun**.

Head down the hallway. Next to an alarm button is a set of double doors that open into the laundry room. Equip the Silenced 9mm and open the laundry room door. Eliminate the male guard waiting inside.

Switch to the dual MiniGuns, then grab the **Box of 12 Ammo** off the laundry room shelf. Go through the single door in the back of the laundry room to the staff locker room. After a few seconds, a female guard walks in. Eliminate her with the dual MiniGuns.

Return to the laundry room and listen for the footsteps of another guard. After he walks by, open the laundry room door and shoot him with the dual MiniGuns, then loot his **44 Special**.

Pick up the guard's body and heft it into the linen closet.

Go back to the locker room and search all the lockers to find a **MedKit** and a **Box of 44 Ammo**. A Floor Plan there reveals the location of Room 41.

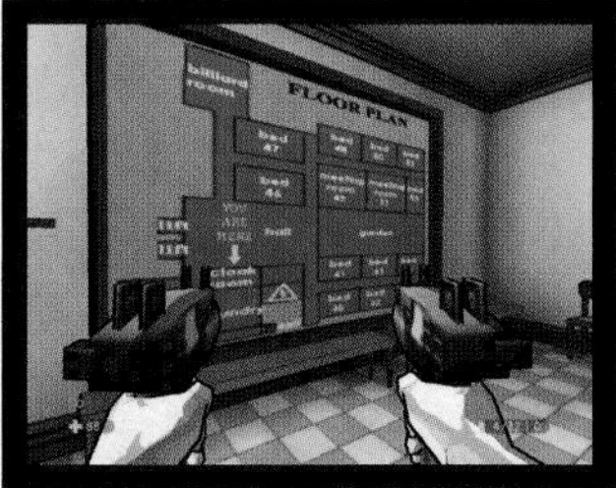

Get the key to Room 41 from the cloakroom, then head back into the hallway. Another guard emerges from Room 42. Eliminate him with the MiniGun, then stash his corpse back in the room he just left. Might as well pick up the **MedKit** while you're there.

Unlock Room 41 with the key, then grab a **Full MedKit** off the bed. Equip the **Shotgun Mike** and aim out the window at Winslow. Follow him with the mike to prepare for your next task.

Mission 25: SECRET MEETINGS

When Willard and the Mongoose arrive, record the conversation.

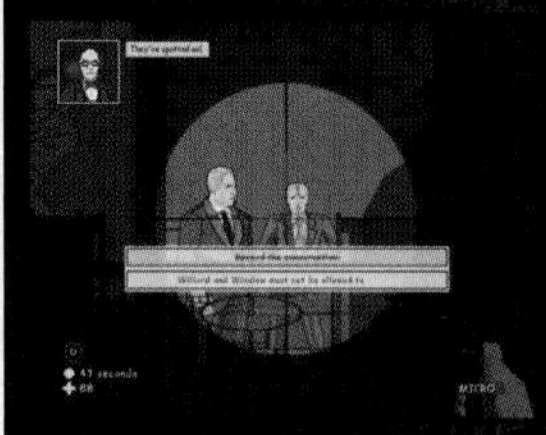

Whoops! They've spotted you, XIII. Cut the power to the elevator to prevent Willard and Winslow from escaping.

Equip the dual MiniGuns and return to the hallway, then run around the corner to the electrical room. Kill the guard in there and throw the switch to shut off the elevator.

CHECKPOINT: NUMBER IX AND NUMBER V.

Head back into the hallway and run to the double doors on the left. Help the FBI agents eliminate any remaining guards, then follow the G-men to the billiard room.

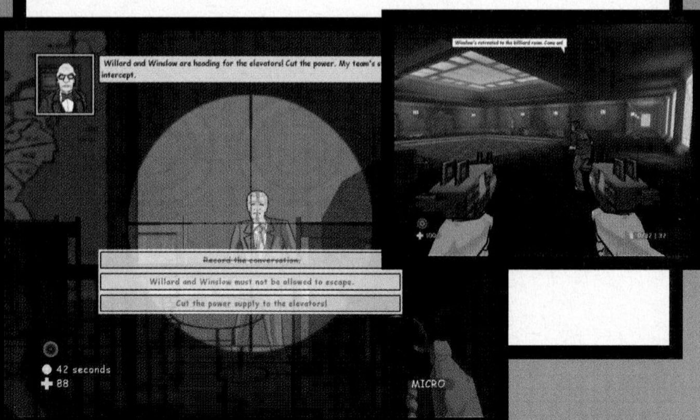

The billiard room is locked, so find another way in, XIII. Go back into the lounge and collect the **MiniGun Ammo** and **Full MedKits** from the bodies of the dead guards. The FBI agent informs you that the billiard room has a glass roof.

Enter the open elevator shaft and climb up the ladder to the vent. Then crawl down the vent to the room above the billiard room.

Shoot out the glass roof, then kill the female guard and Winslow!

BOSS FIGHT: WINSLOW

After busting the glass, remain upstairs and use the MiniGun to target Winslow and the female guard.

Winslow is armed with a Shotgun and he doesn't do much damage as long as you keep your distance.

Your dual MiniGun makes short work of him.

Once Winslow is dead, jump down onto the billiard table and collect the **Documents**, **Shotgun**, and **Key** from his body. Use the Key to open the door.

Willard shoots one of the FBI Agents. He must not get away, XIII. Track him down and kill him!

BOSS FIGHT: WILLARD

Willard is only slightly tougher than Winslow. He is also armed with a shotgun.

As soon as he shoots the FBI Agent, he runs down the hallway and into a meeting room.

Trap him in there, then let him have it with the dual MiniGun.

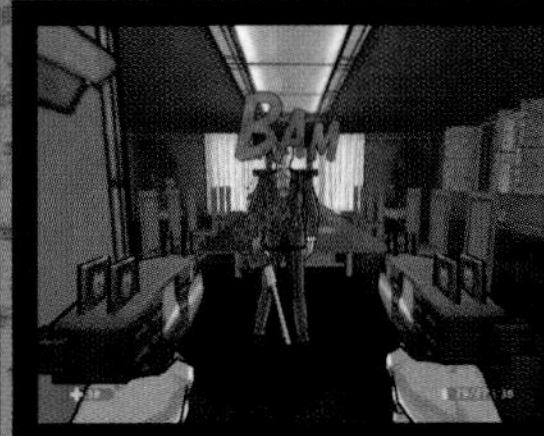

When Willard's dead, collect his documents and the mission ends.

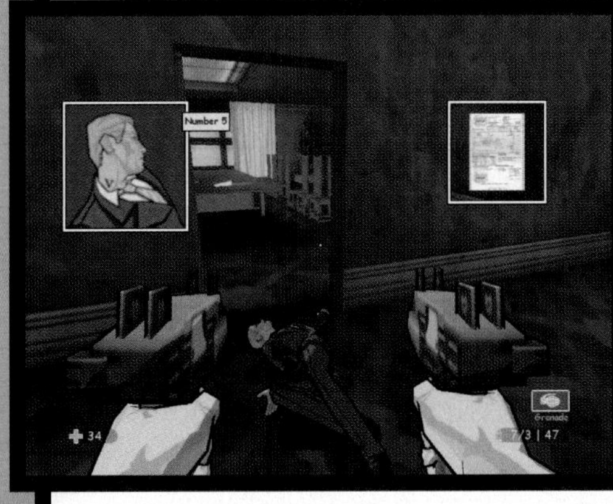

MISSION COMPLETE

Mission 26:

THE SANCTUARY GROUNDS

MISSION BRIEFING

OBJECTIVES

Eliminate the guards without raising the alarm. Infiltrate the sanctuary.

WEAPONS

Throwing Knife	3-Shot Crossbow
9mm	MiniGun
9mm Silencer	Kalash

ENEMIES

Guards

SUMMARY

This is a tough mission, XIII. You must infiltrate the Sanctuary without alerting Number I to your presence. If any of the guards see you, they will radio back to the Sanctuary and the secret meeting will be called off.

QUICK AND DIRTY

Push your way through some bushes and onto the Sanctuary grounds. Use Throwing Knives, stealth, and speed to handle the guards patrolling the hedge maze.

Use the 3-Shot Crossbow to skewer the two guards patrolling the fountain, along with the one near the small pond.

Dive into the pond and smash out the grate at the bottom. Swim through the underwater tunnel to the well.

Climb the ladder in the side of the well, and use the dual MiniGun to shoot the two guards. Find a hole in the fence and climb out onto the cliff ledge.

Use the Grappling Hook to swing across the chasm, then push your way through the bushes. Kill the two guards near the fountains with the 3-Shot Crossbow. Switch back to the dual MiniGun and tear up the three guards in Heavy Body Armor.

Go through the stone arch to the small shrine. Knock over the large cross to reveal an underground passage.

CHECKPOINT: CROSS THE GARDENS

Just to the left of the delivery truck is a place in the bushes where you can push your way through and access the Sanctuary grounds. Use your fists to bash away at the leaves.

Equip a Throwing Knife and peek around the corner to the right. You will hear a guard talking about ordering food for the banquet. When he walks past, sneak up behind him and plug him in the back of the skull with a Throwing Knife.

After the first guard is dead, plow through the hedges to the left. The path goes straight and branches off to the left. You can see the "Tap, Tap, Tap" of a guard walking up the walkway to the left. Use a Throwing Knife to eliminate him.

Move through the hedges until you sense a guard patrolling right near a 'T' junction. There are actually two guards here—one heading off to the left, and the other to the right. You must kill them both very quickly to keep one or the other of them from calling for help. If you choose the right-hand path, you can grab a **9mm** off a bench.

As you move down the path, a guard says, "No, nothing to report. Over." After he makes his radio report, continue along the path and stab him with a Throwing Knife.

The hedge maze ends in a garden area with a fountain. There are two guards patrolling this area. Switch to the 3-Shot Crossbow, then shoot both guards in the head.

Cross the garden and go through the doors. There is a stone stairway leading up. Stand at the bottom of the stairs and zoom in with the Crossbow. Wait there until a guard walks into view, then zap him in the head with a Crossbow Bolt.

At the end of the path is a pond with a metal grate at the bottom. Empty your hands of weapons, then take the plunge. Smash the metal grate and follow it as it drops down into the depths. Swim through the weed-choked tunnel until you see a well with a ladder in the side.

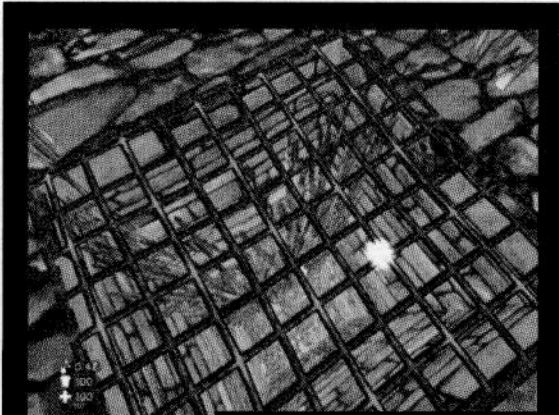

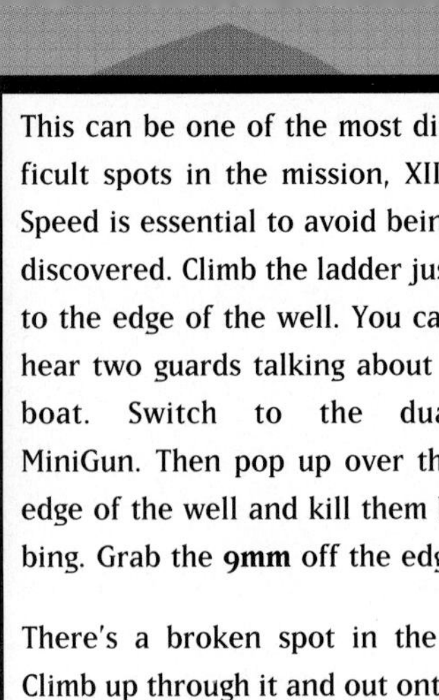

This can be one of the most difficult spots in the mission, XIII. Speed is essential to avoid being discovered. Climb the ladder just to the edge of the well. You can hear two guards talking about a boat. Switch to the dual MiniGun. Then pop up over the edge of the well and kill them both as soon as they quit gabbing. Grab the **9mm** off the edge of the well.

There's a broken spot in the fence surrounding the well. Climb up through it and out onto a ledge on the side of a cliff.

CHECKPOINT: INFILTRATE THE SANCTUARY

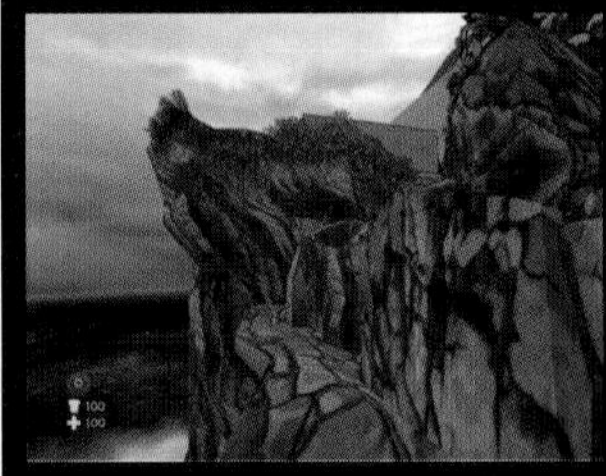

Follow the cliff edge around the corner to where you can see a green and black ring. Use your Grappling Hook to attach to the ring and swing across the chasm to the other side.

Climb the stone steps and then push your way through the bushes with your fists. This is another garden area with two fountains and some trees. A single guard is patrolling the walkway between the trees, while another one walks up and down the steps. Use the 3-Shot Crossbow to kill the guard patrolling between the trees. When the second guard stops at the bottom of the steps, share a Bolt with him, as well.

Move around the fountain and duck behind the bushes. At the top of the steps, you can see a guard wearing a Heavy Helmet and a Heavy Vest. However, there are actually three up there, two of them are out of sight to the left. Since they have on Heavy Helmets, a single Crossbow Bolt will not kill them.

Switch to the dual MiniGun, then charge up the steps. Kill the guard on the right, then run to the left side of the building and waste the other two in quick succession. Speed is essential. If you delay too long, one of the guards will phone in and the meeting will be called off.

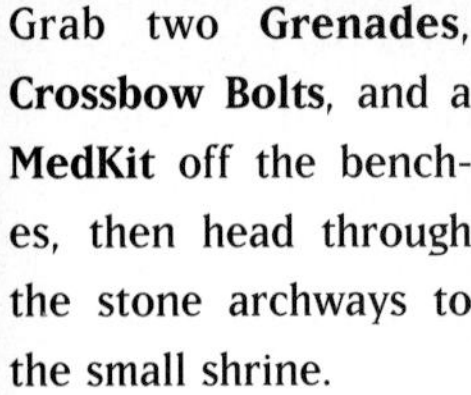

Grab two **Grenades**, **Crossbow Bolts**, and a **MedKit** off the benches, then head through the stone archways to the small shrine.

Walking up to the shrine triggers a flashback.

Inside the shrine is a large plaque on the floor and a similar plaque on the wall. Press the wall plaque to make the floor move a bit. Hmm. It doesn't open, XIII.

Go around behind the altar and look up at the large cross. There's a crack in the base of the cross. Equip the Kalash and shoot this defect until the entire thing topples over and smashes a hole in the plaque on the floor.

Jump down into the hole and walk into the stone hallway to complete the mission.

MISSION COMPLETE

Mission 27:

THE BANQUET HALL

MISSION BRIEFING

OBJECTIVES

Find the place where the Clan of 20 meet up. Do not attract the attention of the Clan members.

WEAPONS

Throwing Knives
9mm
9mm Silencer
3-Shot Crossbow
Kalash
MiniGun

ENEMIES

Guards

SUMMARY

Superb work sneaking into the Sanctuary, XIII. Now that you're inside, discreetly eliminate any guards you encounter and find the secret passage leading to the meeting place of the Clan of 20.

QUICK AND DIRTY

Climb the ladder and eliminate the two guards in the briefing room. Go out onto the balcony and use Throwing Knives or the 3-Shot Crossbow to eliminate all the guards in this area.

Ascend the stairs, then head into a long hallway with a red carpet. Killing the guard gets you a Key.

Go back across the balcony and open the metal gate with the Key. Collect the Magnetic Card from a desk in the small office.

Return to the hallway with the red carpet, open the gallery door with the Magnetic Card and eliminate the two guards.

Find the Stone Key hidden in the wall in the art supply room, then kill the two guards who try to stop you.

Use the Stone Key on the monument to open the secret passage.

CHECKPOINT: BEHIND ENEMY LINES

Climb the ladder into the Sanctuary. If you look through the window in the door up ahead, you can see two guards posted in the briefing room.

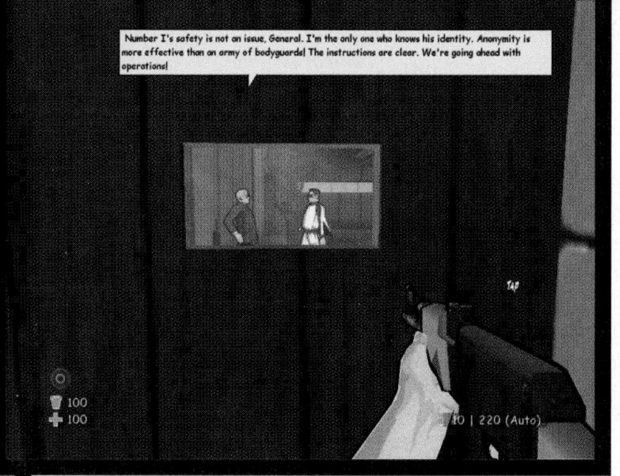

Open the door and eliminate both guards with the 3-Shot Crossbow. Be quick so they can't sound the alarm, then exit the opposite door and sprint down the hallway.

Equip a Throwing Knife and open the door to catch a guard with his back to you. Deal him that Throwing Knife in the back of his head.

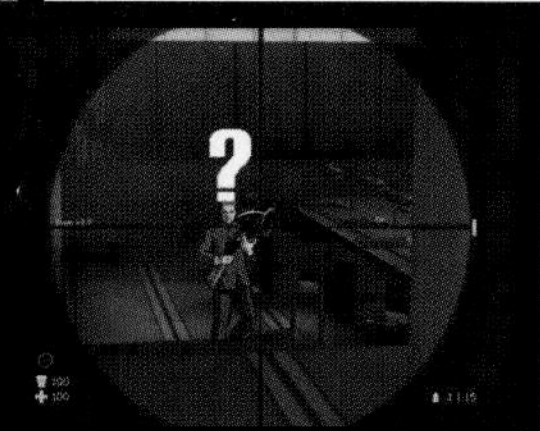

CHECKPOINT: ON THE BALCONY

Walk out onto the balcony and turn to your right. After a few seconds, another guard comes into view. Take him out with a Throwing Knife.

Up the stairway, you will see another guard armed with a Crossbow. Equip the 3-Shot Crossbow and kill him when he walks out from behind the stone pillars.

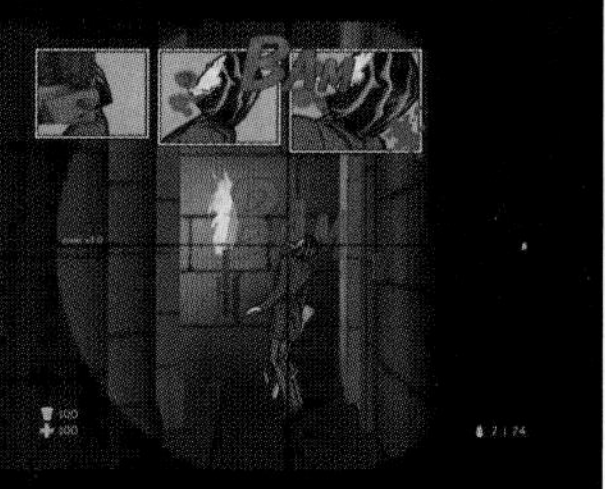

Walk up the stairs and turn to the left. Zoom in with the Crossbow and wait until a female guard walks into view, then hit her with a Crossbow Bolt.

Go down the balcony to the short hallway where the female guard just walked. Open the door into a hallway with a red carpet. A single guard is musing about having left his Magnetic Card behind.

Eliminate this guy with a Crossbow Bolt, then search his body to find a **Key**.

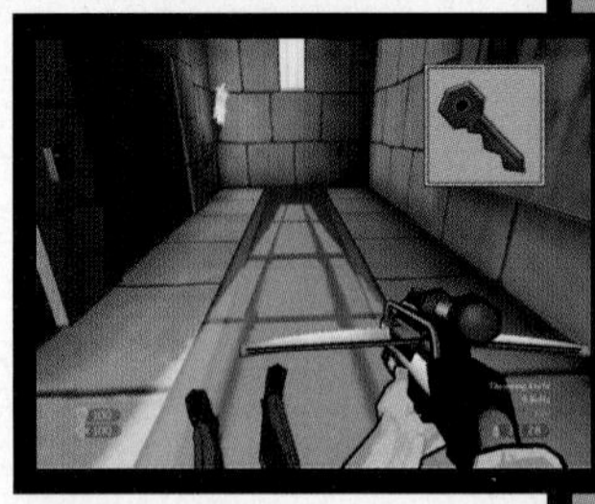

Right across from the door with the Magnetic Lock, is a doorway leading back out onto the balcony. Open that door and walk up the stairs.

There's an iron gate at the end of the balcony. Use the **Key** you just got from the dead guard to open it. Enter the small office and grab the **Magnetic Key** out of the desk drawer.

Head back down the stairs and open the door with your Magnetic Card.

Two guards are in a gallery below talking. Make sure your 3-Shot Crossbow is loaded with all three Bolts, then shoot the guard who's talking. Target the second guard and impale him before he can sound the alarm.

Go downstairs into the gallery. There is a stone monument here featuring a familiar symbol... with one piece missing.

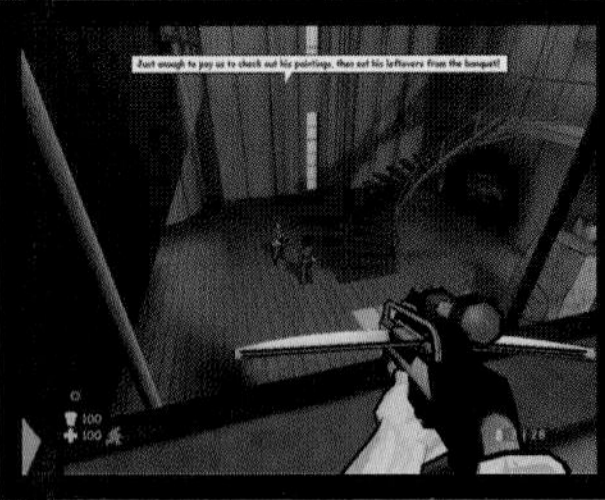

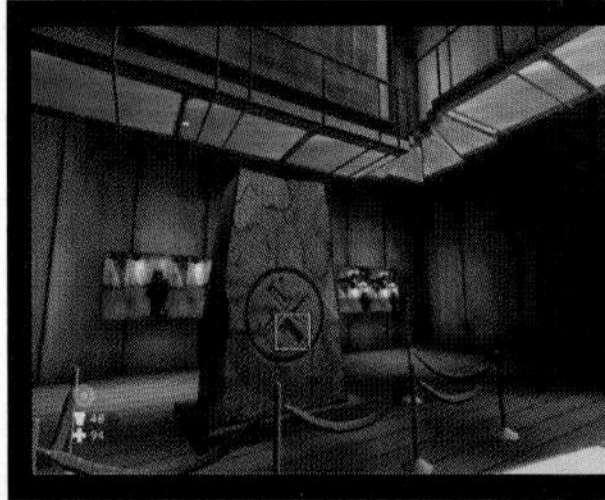

Behind the stairway is a doorway leading to a small art supply storage room. Take the **Full MedKit** from the table. There are some loose stones in the wall. Pull them aside and collect the **Documents** and the **Stone Key**.

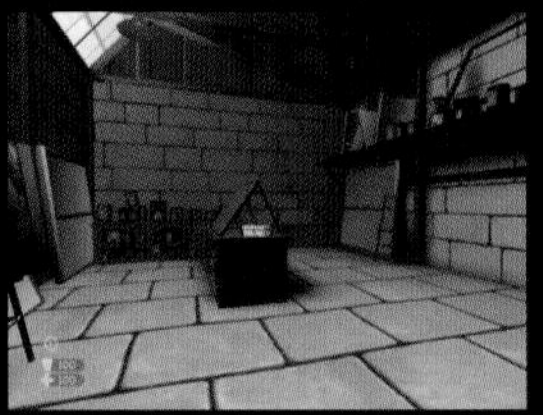

As soon as you obtain the Documents and the Stone Key, two female guards come running. Switch to the dual MiniGun and eliminate the first guard as she runs into the room.

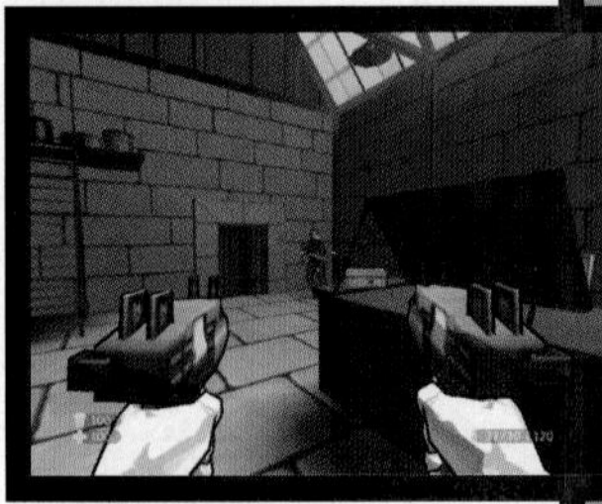

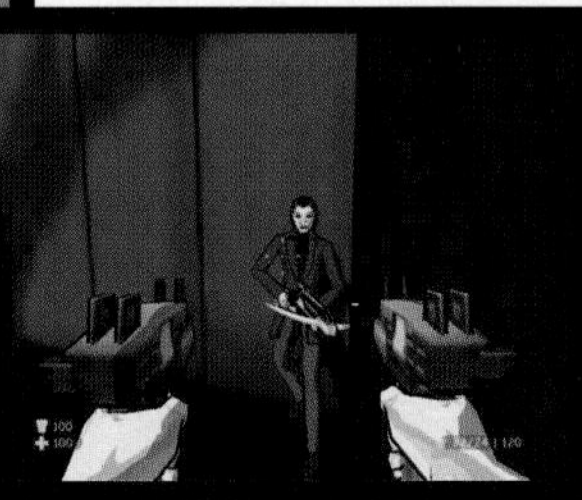

The second female guard is waiting for you out in the gallery. Look to your right as you enter the gallery to spot her.

Use the **Stone Key** on the monument to open the secret passage in the corner of the room, then dash in to end the mission.

MISSION COMPLETE

Mission 28:
BENEATH THE SANCTUARY

MISSION BRIEFING

OBJECTIVES

Spy on the meeting. Eliminate the guards without raising the alarm.

WEAPONS

Throwing Knife	3-Shot Crossbow
9mm	Kalash
9mm Silencer	MiniGun

ENEMIES

Guards

SUMMARY

You are now in the caverns under the Sanctuary, XIII. Eliminate the guards without raising the alarm, then spy on the secret meeting to find out Number I's secret plan.

QUICK AND DIRTY

Explore the caverns beneath the Sanctuary. Kill any guards you find without raising an alarm.

Use the Grappling Hook on the second ring in the underground chamber to pull yourself up onto the ledge.

Eliminate the guards in the chamber below, and then jump down to the chamber floor. Kill the two guards at the end of the hall, then exit the hallway through the side door.

Head up the stairs and use your Lockpick on all the doors blocking your progress. Continue to eliminate all the guards you encounter.

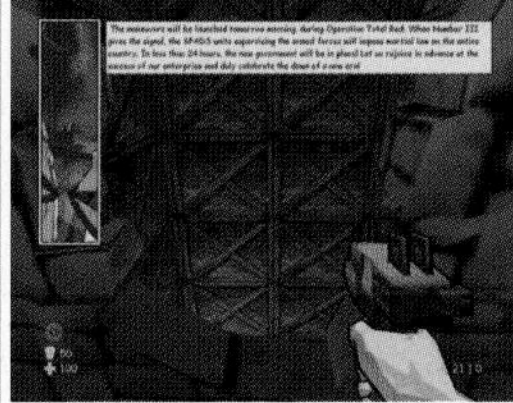

Jump down into the crawlspace next to the bell tower and listen in on the Clan of 20's secret meeting.

When the meeting is over, use the Grappling Hook on the bell to lower yourself down to the meeting hall.

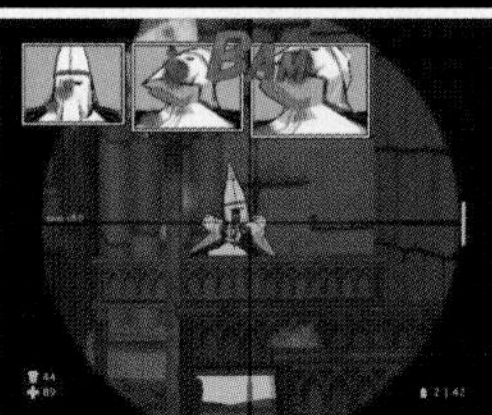

Eliminate the Clan members who try to block your way. Use the Lockpick on the side door and fight your way up onto the balcony.

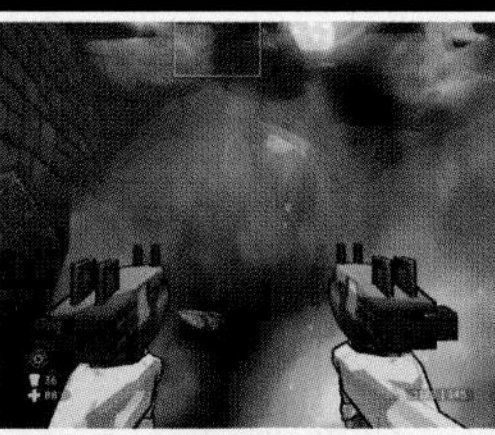

Use the Grappling Hook on the ring above the balcony to swing across to another balcony before the Sanctuary burns to the ground.

Fight your way through the hallways and exit the Sanctuary onto the cliff.

CHECKPOINT: IN THE DUNGEON

This is a damp and foggy underground, XIII. The area is heavily patrolled by guards. Watch for the "Tap, Tap, Tap" of their footsteps.

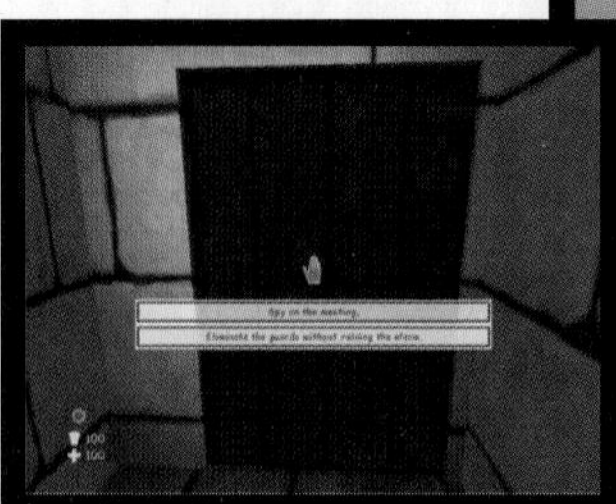

This is a good place to use the **Silence 9mm**. Pass through the doorway and enter the hallway. Kill the female guard, then the two male guards talking just around the corner.

Enter the cavern area and eliminate the male guard with his back to you. A female guard comes running when she sees the body. Take care of her before she can sound an alarm.

There are two places to attach your Grappling Hook in the cavern ceiling. Use the hook on the first ring to pull yourself up to the ledge. Kill the guard in the stone hallway, and then search the three rooms to obtain a **Crossbow**, **Crossbow Bolts**, **Throwing Knives**, a **MedKit**, and an **Important Document**.

Follow the hallway around to a ledge above the cavern floor. Use the Hook to swing across to the opposite ledge, then grab the **MedKit**.

Go into the stone hallway. You can hear two guards talking up ahead. More **Crossbow Bolts** are behind the first door. Use your **Lockpick** on the second door to unlock a room containing two **MiniGuns** and a **MedKit**.

A pair of guards are talking in a chamber below you. Equip the 3-Shot Crossbow and eliminate the first guard when he enters the chamber, then move out onto the ledge and shoot through the stone archway to kill his buddy.

Jump across to the ledge with the **Full MedKit**, hop down to a second ledge, then again to the floor. Enter the chamber with all the pillars. You can see two more guards ahead in front of two large doors. Use the 3-Shot Crossbow to spear the light-haired guard first, then set your aim on his dark-haired companion.

There's a small door and a stairway leading up behind two torches. Use the **Lockpick** on the door at the top of the stairs.

Go down the hall and use the Lockpick on the next door—a female guard is on the other side, and a male guard is in a side room. Eliminate them both, then collect the **Light Vest**.

Use the Lockpick on the door at the top of the stairs. Eliminate the male guard behind this door, then ascend several stairways. Jump down into a narrow hallway and look out through the hole in the wall.

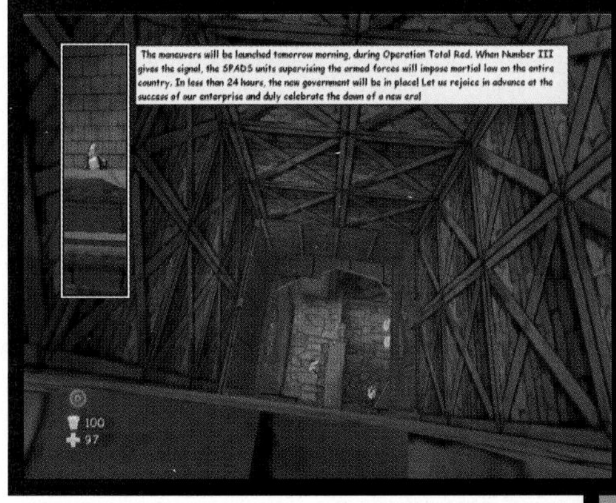

Below the bell tower you can hear the **Clan of 20** holding their secret meeting. When the meeting is over, Colonel Amos radios in that it's safe for you to leave the Sanctuary.

CHECKPOINT: ESCAPE FROM THE SANCTUARY

Connect the Grappling Hook to the bottom of the bell and lower yourself all the way to the meeting hall floor. Disconnect the Hook, then duck down behind the altar.

Equip the 3-Shot Crossbow and eliminate the two robed Clan members at the end of the hall. Duck down and reload the Crossbow, then eliminate the two Clan members who appear in the upper balconies.

Equip the dual MiniGun and run to the end of the hall. The chamber begins to catch fire! Use the Lockpick on the side door.

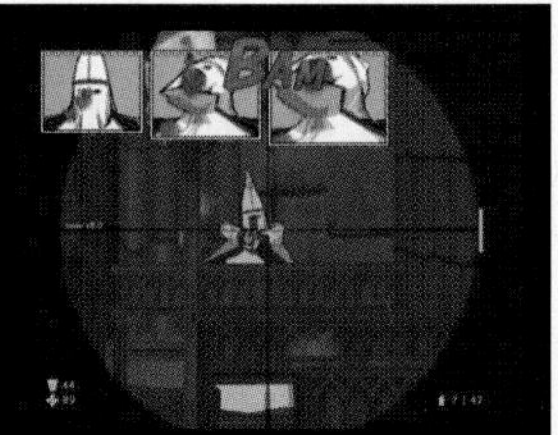

Run down the long hallway and through the small door. When you turn the corner you will see two Clan members. Fire your MiniGun at them, then run out onto the balcony.

The meeting hall is now fully ablaze. Connect the Grappling Hook to the ring in the ceiling and swing over to the other balcony.

Run down the hallways, wasting two more Clan members as you go. Enter a side door to complete the mission.

MISSION COMPLETE

Mission 29:
THE GREAT ESCAPE

MISSION BRIEFING

OBJECTIVES

Run to the end of the cliff!

WEAPONS

Throwing Knife
9mm
9mm Silencer
Crossbow
Kalash
MiniGun
Grenades

ENEMIES

Guards
Clan of 20 Members

SUMMARY

This is a simple mission, XIII. Run for your life!

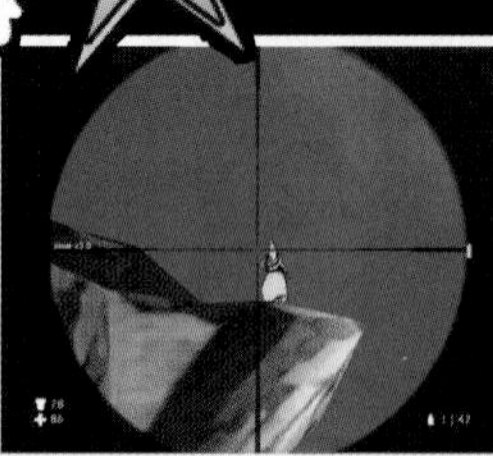

Run along the cliff edge and eliminate any Clan of 20 members or guards who get in your way. Use the Grappling Hook to pull yourself up the side of the cliff.

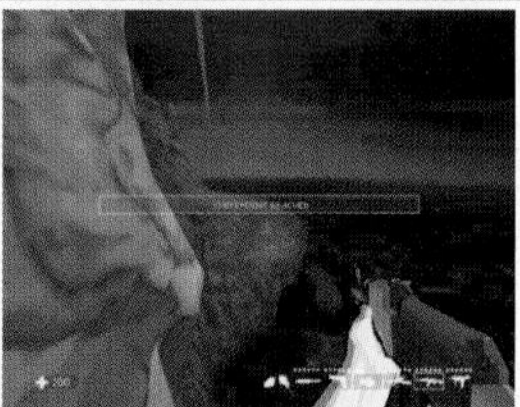

Ride the wire assemblies across the gaps. Keep shooting as you slide down the wires.

Four helicopters attack, preventing a rescue chopper from picking you up. Shoot the gunners in the helicopters to drive them off.

Jump off the cliff like an action hero, and grab the ladder dangling from the helicopter. Hoo-Aaah!

CHECKPOINT: OUTSIDE SANCTUARY

Check all your weapons as soon as the mission begins, XIII. Reload each one so it has a full load of ammo.

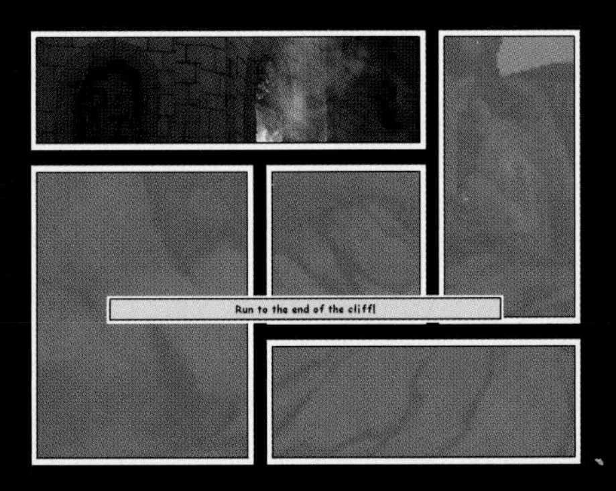

Equip the 3-Shot Crossbow and start running down the cliff. Ahead is a hook you can use to pull yourself up the cliff face. Use the 3-Shot Crossbow to eliminate the Clan member at the bottom of the cliff, along with his colleague sporting the Kalash at the top.

Use theGrappling Hook to hoist yourself up the cliff, then jump over to the cliff, equip the Kalash, and eliminate the first guard. Duck behind the cliff wall and switch to the 3-Shot Crossbow. Way off up on the cliff wall you can see another Clan member. Nail him with the 3-Shot Crossbow, then switch back to the Kalash.

There is a wire assembly up ahead you can use to cross the gap. Kill the Clan member with the Kalash as you slide down the wire. Brace yourself for an explosion up at the Sanctuary that will send a Clan member flying out of the building!

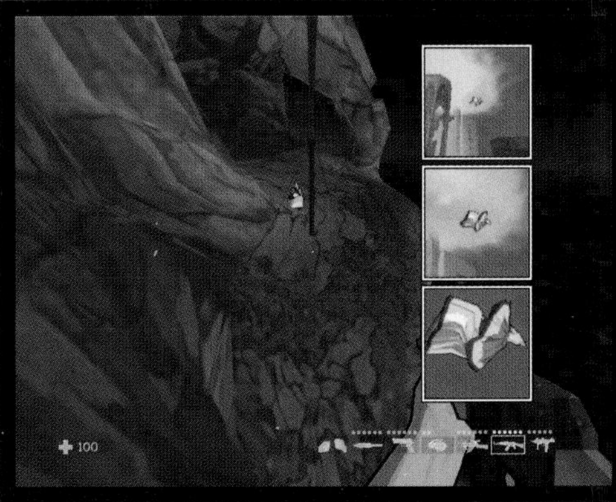

Use the Kalash to kill the Clan member and the guard under the stone arch. Reload and then ride the next wire assembly across the second gap.

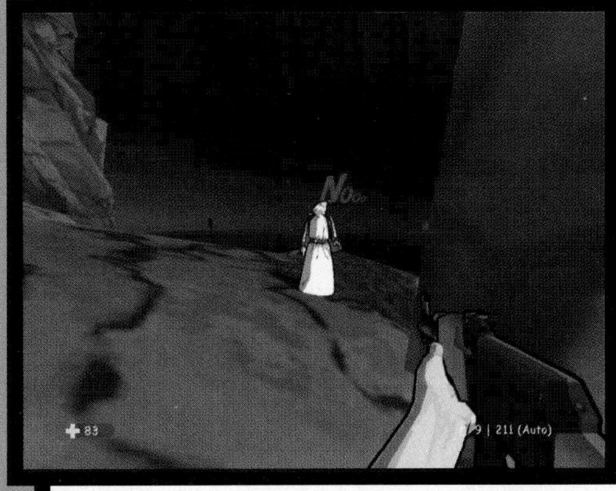

CHECKPOINT: HELICOPTERS ATTACK!

Amos radios in that they are sending a rescue chopper for you. As you ride the wire across the gap, use the Kalash or the 3-Shot Crossbow to greet the two guards waiting for you.

As soon as you hit the ground, switch to the dual MiniGuns and start shooting at the guards who come running around the cliff edge.

Four enemy helicopters attack. Use the Kalash on these whirlibirds so the rescue chopper can pick you up.

BOSS FIGHT: FOUR HELICOPTERS

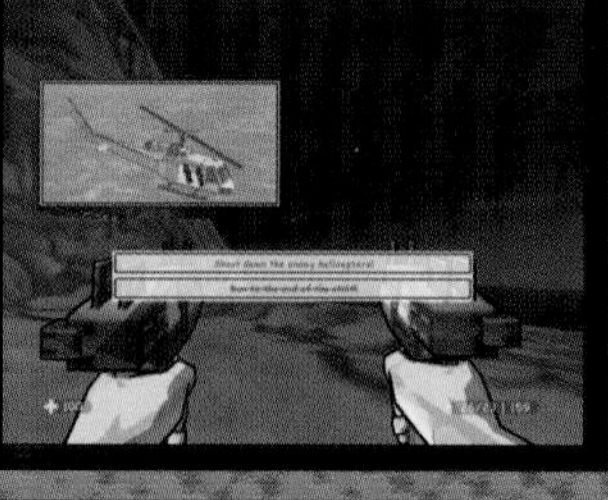

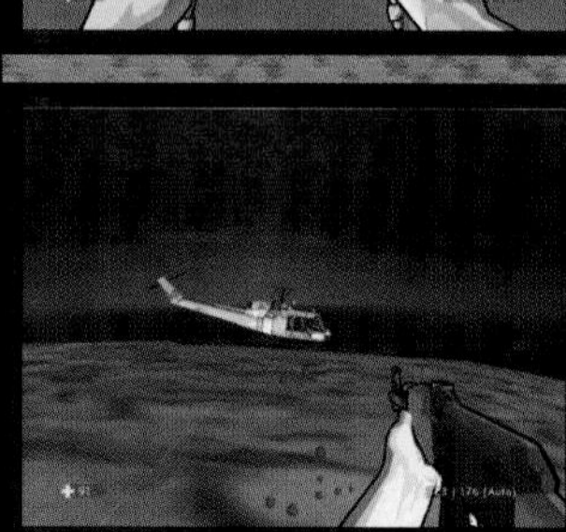

You are attacked by four helicopters, and there is nowhere to hide!

Dodge to the left and right to avoid being hit by the gunners in the helicopter's bay.

Focus your shots at the guards firing at you rather than simply firing on the actual helicopters. Once the guards inside are dead, the helicopter will fly off.

When the four helicopters retreat, the rescue chopper will arrive. Jump from the cliff edge and grab onto the ladder to end the mission.

MISSION COMPLETE

Mission 30:
SSH SECRET BASE

MISSION BRIEFING

OBJECTIVES

Infiltrate the secret SSH1 base. Avoid being spotted. Neutralize the GIs.

WEAPONS

9mm

Assault Rifle

ENEMIES

GIs

SUMMARY

Senator Sheridan will try to sneak you into the SSH secret base disguised as Colonel Marshall. When that fails, you will need to find another way into the base.

QUICK AND DIRTY

Follow Senator Sheridan to the base door. When you are turned away, find another way into the base.

Enter the locker room and subdue the GIs. Knock out the security booth GI. Open the Vault door and get the Magnetic Key. Knock out the lobby GI and head down to Security Level Blue.

Sneak up behind the GIs and knock them out, then hide the bodies. When you have subdued them all, take the elevator down to Security Level Orange.

Continue to use chairs and push brooms to neutralize all the GIs, then hide in the bathroom until President Galbrain leaves.

Knock out the last GI in the meeting room. Enter the steam tunnels to end the mission.

CHECKPOINT: SSH1 FRONT GATE

Follow Senator Sheridan to the front security gate. You are turned away at the entrance and escorted back out of the high security area by an armed GI. General Carrington will radio that you need to find another way into the base.

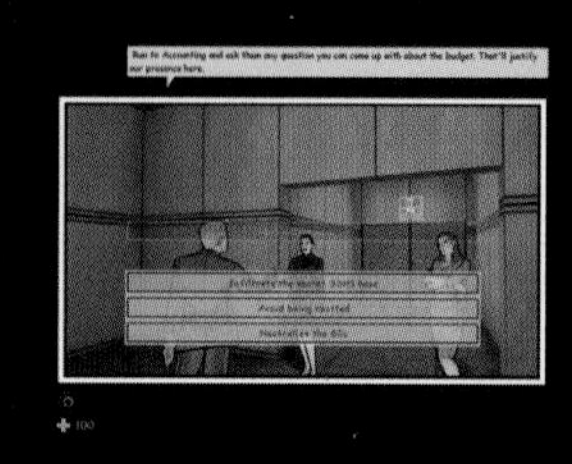

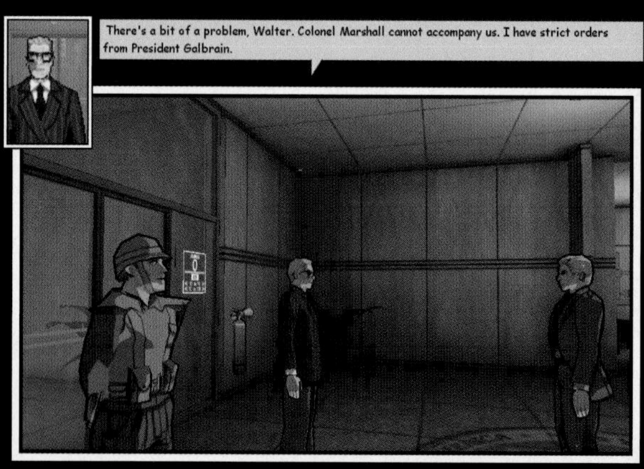

As you return to the base entrance, a GI leaves the locker room on his way to the candy machine. Looks like a good chance for you to sneak into the base, XIII. Enter the locker room as the GI walks out.

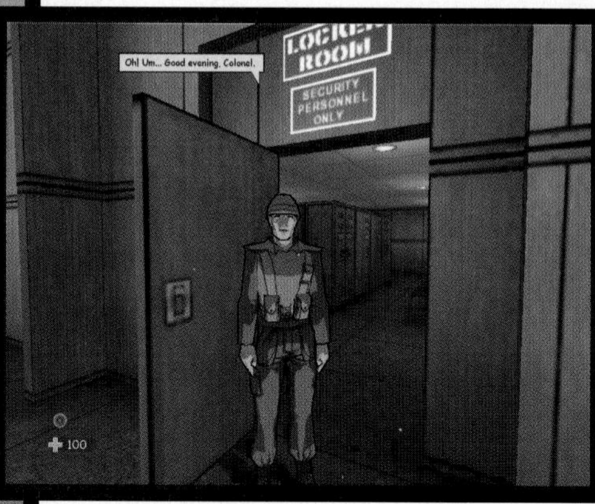

There are two GIs in the locker room, one is getting things out of his locker and another is standing in front of the mirror. Move up behind each GI and grab them. Hit Action again to knock them unconscious.

Take the push broom from the locker room and exit the side door. You can see a GI in the control room through the back door. Hang back a little and watch until you see the GI in the lobby move out of sight, then open the control room door and bash the GI on the head with your broom.

Hit the red buttons to open the security door and grab the **Magnetic Card**. Exit the control room and close the door behind you before the GI guarding the lobby starts making his rounds again.

Grab a chair from the locker room, then duck down and head over to the security door. Open the door with the Magnetic Card. Wait until the GI in the lobby makes his rounds and turns his back, then walk up behind him and bash him on the back of the head with a chair.

Use the Magnetic Card to open the large Vault security door that leads down to the Blue Security Level.

CHECKPOINT: BLUE SECURITY LEVEL

As you descend the stairs you sense the movement of the GI below. Keep an eye on your sense windows—they will let you know when it's safe to move.

When the GI at the bottom of the stairs moves to the right, sneak up behind him and knock him out. Grab his body and drag it into the generator room.

Take the chair out of the generator room and head toward the end of the hallway. As you proceed, you sense the next GI. Wait until he gets close by then turns around. Once he has his back turned, hit him over the head with the chair.

Drag the body back to the generator room. Snag another chair from the hallway and use the same tactic on the next GI.

After you knock out the third GI, grab his body and hide it in the nearest generator room. Then grab the chair in the generator room and wait a few seconds. A fourth GI patrolling the hallway walks past. Sneak up behind him and smack him with the chair.

Take the push broom from behind the electrical box in the hallway. You can see the access door and a security booth at the end of the hall. There's also a set of double doors just before the security booth. Open them and wait behind the electrical box until you sense that the GI in the hallway has turned his back, then bash him with the broom.

There is another push broom in this hallway. Take it and enter the security booth through the back door. Knock the GI out and hit the button that opens the security doors.

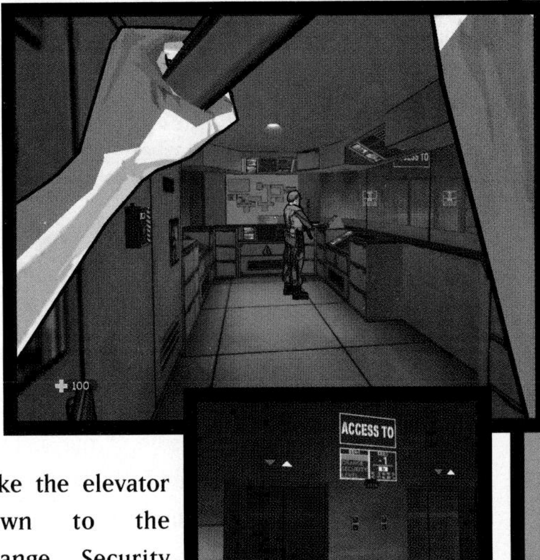

Take the elevator down to the Orange Security Level.

CHECKPOINT: ORANGE SECURITY LEVEL

Up ahead you can see a security booth. Go through the double doors behind the security booth and walk up to the corner. You sense a GI heading your direction and walking into a locker room.

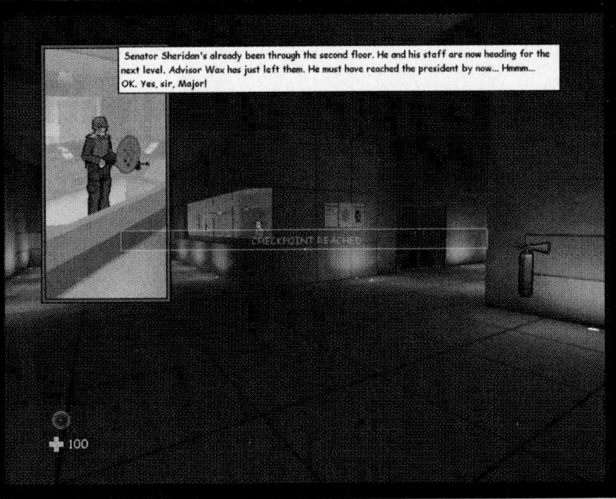

Follow the GI into the locker room and knock him out with a push broom. Grab an ashtray off one of the benches and return to the security booth. Knock the GI in the security booth senseless by tossing the ashtray at his head.

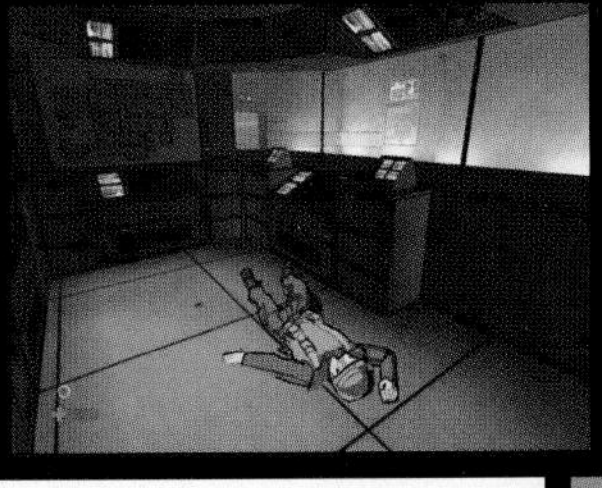

Straight down the hall you can see a GI on patrol. When he moves out of sight, go down the hallway and hide behind the electrical box. Grab the push broom. You will sense two GIs patrolling the next hallway.

When the guard at the far end of the hallway has his back turned, knock out the GI closest to you. Then grab his body and duck back around the corner, out of sight.

Keep an eye on the GI at the far end of the hall. Whenever he turns his back, run down the hall. When he starts to turn back around, duck behind the electrical boxes. When you get close to him, wait until he turns his back one more time, then render him unconscious.

Grab another push broom or chair and head down the hallway to the area just outside the double doors. You will sense a guard approaching the coffee machine.

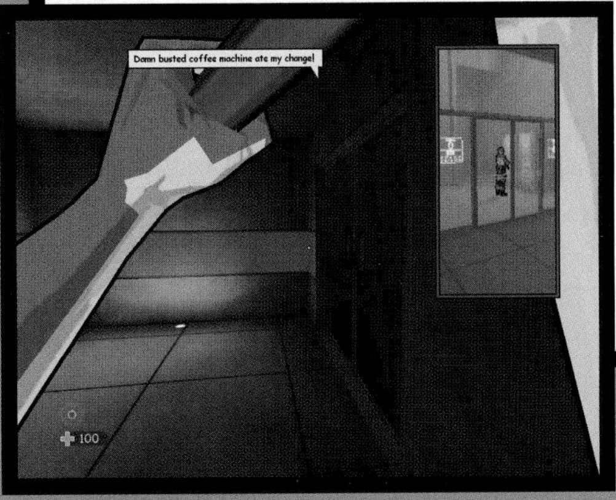

This is a bit tricky, XIII. You must act quickly. While the GI is trying to get his change out of the coffee machine, go through the double doors and the glass doors, then run up behind the GI and knock him out.

Grab his body and walk through the door on the left and into the restroom. Drop the body out of sight, then pick up a push broom.

Outside you sense that President Galbrain has left the meeting room. After a few seconds a GI heads for the restroom. When he opens the door, knock him out and hide his body.

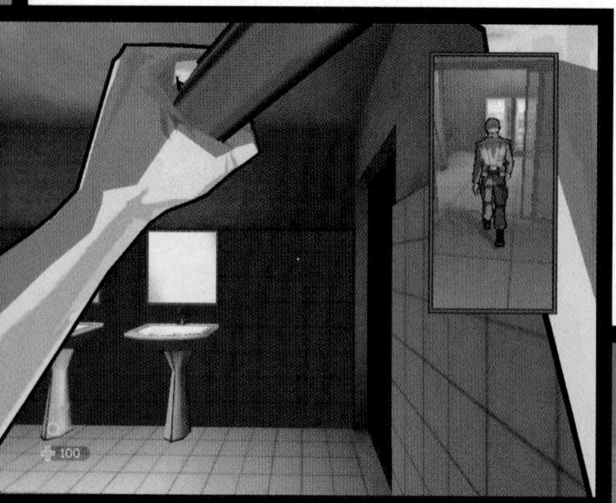

Grab the push broom from the lobby and enter the glass doors into the meeting room. The GI in there has his back to you. Knock him out.

There's a door on the other side of the meeting room that leads to a room filled with steam pipes. Enter this room to finish the mission.

MISSION COMPLETE

Mission 31:
THE SPADS ATTACK

MISSION BRIEFING

OBJECTIVES

Avoid being spotted. Neutralize the GIs.

WEAPONS

9mm
Assault Rifle
Shotgun
MiniGun

ENEMIES

GIs
SPADS Soldiers
General Standwell

SUMMARY

You are an expert at dodging GIs, XIII. Neutralize a few more, then load up with weapons and ammo from the armory. Defeat the SPADS soldiers and General Standwell. Rescue President Galbrain.

CHECKPOINT: THE ARMORY

Pick up the push broom and wait until the GI outside has finished radioing in. Open the door, and then knock him out.

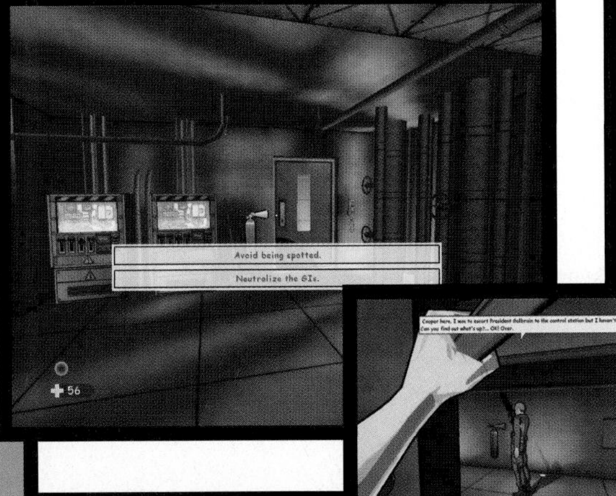

QUICK AND DIRTY

Knock out three GIs in the hallway and then the one GI in the Armory. Load up with weapons, ammo, and body armor.

Go into the conference room and fight off five SPADS soldiers.

Eliminate General Standwell!

Rescue the President and open the Conference Room doors. Fight off a few more SPADS soldiers, then leave the President with a GI for safety.

Assist the GIs in fighting the SPADS soldiers. A GI will open the Vault door to Security Level Red.

There's a chair right at the end of the hall. Pick it up and knock out the next GI you encounter, then grab another chair and knock out the third GI.

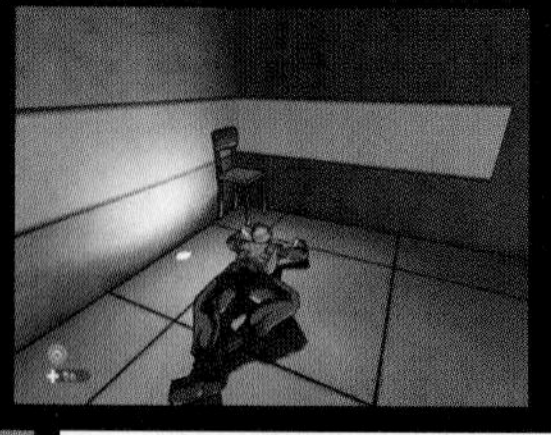

Take another chair and look in the Armory window. Wait until the GI inside has his back turned, then knock him out. Start loading up with weapons and ammo. You can grab a **Full MedKit**, **Heavy Vest**, **AR Grenades**, **MiniGun**, two **Boxes of 12 Ammo**, and two **Boxes of MiniGun Ammo**.

Equip the Assault Rifle, then go into the Conference Room. It seems a little quiet out here, XIII. Be on guard. The SPADS have taken control of the base!

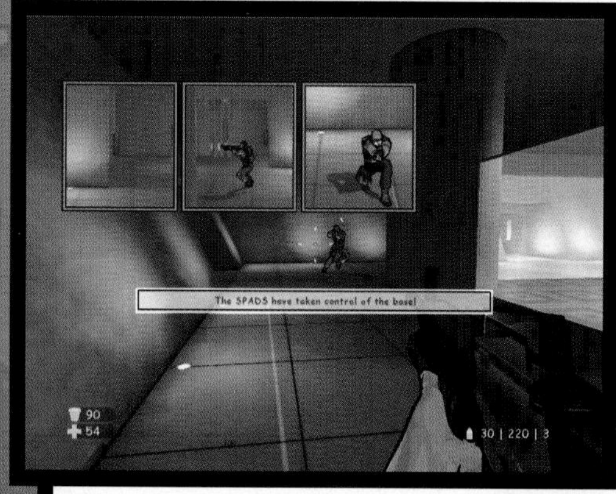

You are attacked by five SPADS soldiers. Dodge around the pillars and use the side rooms as cover while you eliminate these troops.

As soon as the SPADS are dead, General Standwell emerges from a side room and attacks. Kill the general!

BOSS FIGHT: GENERAL STANDWELL

General Standwell may have only one eye, but he's a great shot, XIII. He's also armed with a M60 machine gun.

With limited MedKits in this area, you must make every shot count. Dodge around the pillars and dump two clips from the Assault Rifle into the general to soften him up.

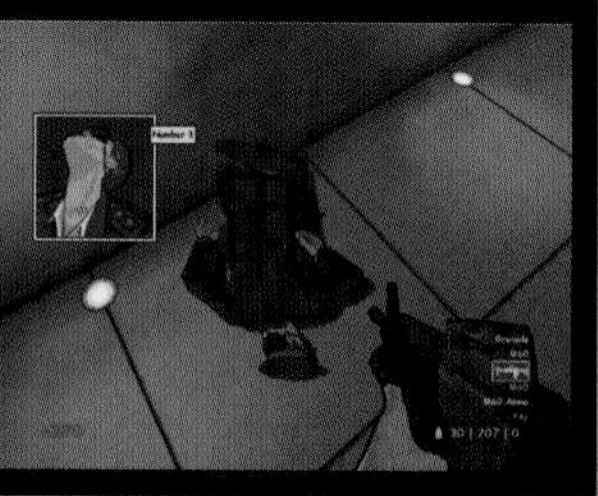

Once you've done some damage, run back and give yourself some distance. Finish him off with AR Grenades.

When General Standwell is dead, collect his **M60** machine gun and his **Key**. Unlock the door marked 'Security Personnel Only'. President Galbrain is inside.

Protect the President and entrust him to a GI. Hit the button in the security room to open the doors. Pick up President Galbrain and exit the conference room.

CHECKPOINT: PROTECT THE PRESIDENT

Set the President down after you exit the conference room. Equip the **M60** and walk around the corner. As you head down the hall you see Senator Sheridan and his assistants walk by on an upper level, prisoners of the SPADS. A SPADS soldier behind them notices you and shoots out the glass.

Duck back behind the corner, then pop out just enough to kill the SPADS soldier coming out of the side door. Duck back behind the corner again, then equip a **Grenade**. Peek out again and throw the Grenade to the end of the hallway where more SPADS soldiers are waiting.

Leave the President there and walk down the side hallway to the restroom. Kill the SPADS soldier inside, then grab the two **Grenades** and **AR Ammo** off the table.

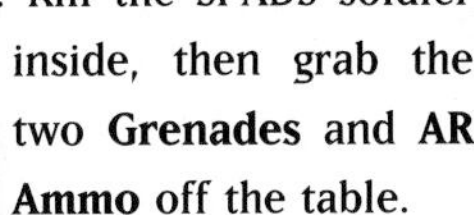

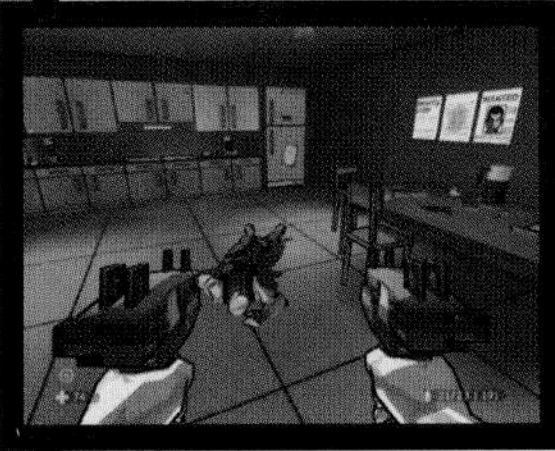

There's a locker room at the end of the hall. Kill the SPADS soldier inside and grab a **MedKit** off the wall and a **Light Vest** off a bench.

Go back and pick up the President, then continue down the hallway until you meet up with the GI. Leave the President with the GI.

Help the GIs fight off the four SPADS soldiers. Use **Grenades** on the SPADS behind the tables to make it a quick fight.

When the fight is over, the GI opens the Vault door to the Red Security Level. Enter it to end the mission.

MISSION COMPLETE

Mission 32:
OPERATION TOTAL RED

MISSION BRIEFING

OBJECTIVES

Stop Operation Total Red.

WEAPONS

9mm
Shotgun
Assault Rifle
MiniGun
M60
Grenades

ENEMIES

SPADS Soldiers
Army Soldiers

SUMMARY

Could Wax be Number 1? Eliminate the SPADS soldiers in SSH1's control center to stop Operation Total Red. Free Senator Sheridan.

QUICK AND DIRTY

Enter the Armory across from the computer control center and load up with weapons and ammo. Use the Lockpick to open the Control Room.

Eliminate all the SPADS and Army soldiers in the control room.

Confront Wax, then grab his Magnetic Key to free Senator Sheridan. The Senator will open the Missile Bunker Vault door.

CHECKPOINT: RED SECURITY LEVEL

As you enter the Red Security Level, you see Senator Sheridan and his assistants trapped in a computer control room. Across the hall is a door that leads to the Armory. Enter the Armory and load up with a **Light Helmet**, **Box of M60 Ammo**, **Box of AR Ammo**, two **Full MedKits**, **Heavy Vest**, **MiniGun**, **Grenades**, **Shotguns**, **M60s**, and **Assault Rifles**.

Pick the lock on the double doors with the **Lockpick**. When you open the door, you can see that the control room is infested with SPADS.

Go through the glass doors into the control room and kill all the SPADS with the M60. More SPADS soldiers and Army soldiers attack from the upper levels, from the side doors, and from a stairway on the side of the room.

Up the stairs. Wax has locked himself into the control room and set the Nuclear Weapons in the base to explode. Climb the stairs on the right to confront Wax.

Wax meets a grisly end. Enter the control room and collect his **Magnetic Card**. Head back down the stairs and use the Magnetic Card to free Senator Sheridan and his assistants.

After Senator Sheridan opens the Vault door, enter the Missile Bunker to end the mission.

MISSION COMPLETE

Mission 33:

SELF-DESTRUCT IN TWO MINUTES

MISSION BRIEFING

OBJECTIVES

Cancel the base's self-destruct procedure.

WEAPONS

- 9mm
- Shotgun
- Assault Rifle
- MiniGun
- M60
- Grenades

ENEMIES

The Mongoose

SUMMARY

You have only two minutes to reach the Control Room and shut down the self-destruct sequence, XIII. Make every second count.

QUICK AND DIRTY

Run onto the missile platform and use the crane to cross the missile bay. When the crane stops halfway across, use the Grappling Hook to swing to the other side.

Enter the restroom and the locker room. Shoot the United States map to climb into the vent, then drop down into the control room.

There's a bomb wired to the control panel. Use the Lockpick to exit the control room. Use the Lockpick again on the computer room door. Shoot off the lock on the computer room cage.

Shoot all the computers in the computer room to shut down the self-destruct sequence.

Leave the computer room and enter the Armory to load up with weapons. Climb down the ladder onto the missile bay floor.

Fight the Mongoose!

Climb the ladder out of the missile bay and meet with Jones, General Carrington, and Senator Sheridan.

CHECKPOINT: TWO MINUTE WARNING

When the Vault door opens, run onto the missile platform. Throw the switch on the crane to move over the missiles.

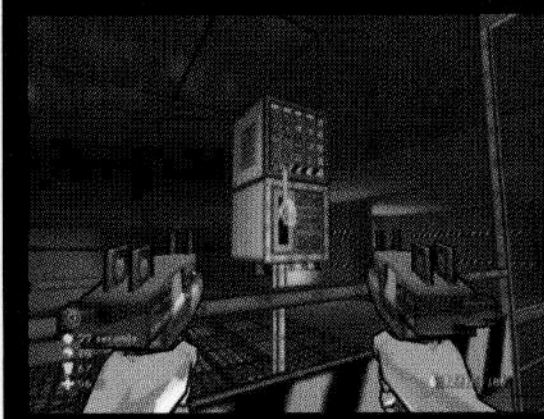

As the crane approaches the missiles, equip the Grappling Hook. The crane stops before completely crossing the missile bay. Use the Hook to swing across to the other side.

Run down the hallway marked 'Control Room'. Up ahead you can see the security door closing. Too late!

Enter the restroom, then head right to the locker room. Inside, shoot the map of the United States to break the grate behind it.

Jump up onto the bench, then duck down and climb into the vent. Shoot out the grate on the other end and drop down into the control room.

'This is not good.' Wax has wired the control panel with a bomb. If you try to turn off the self-destruct, it will explode.

Follow the wires with your eyes, XIII. It looks like they lead to an electrical room just up a short flight of stairs.

Use the Lockpick on the door at the top of the stairs, then again on the computer room door.

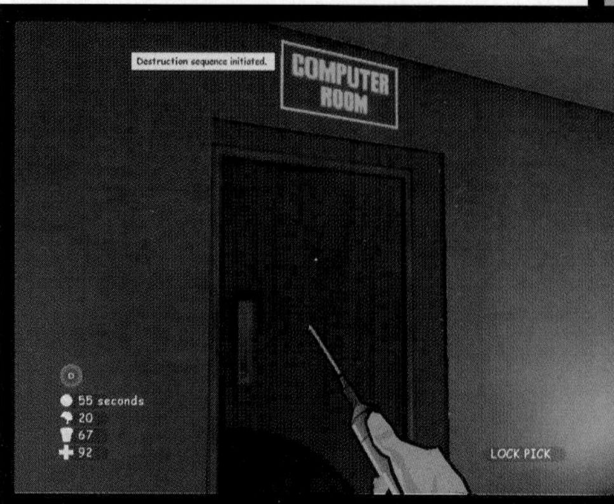

The computer room cage is locked with a heavy lock. No time for Lockpicks, XIII. Equip the Assault Rifle and shoot off the lock.

Use the Assault Rifle to destroy all the computers in the computer room to stop the self-destruct. Whew!

Exit the computer room and head left down the hall. Throw the switch to open the heavy-duty security door.

Pick up some extra gear on your way out. Enter the restroom and get the **Full MedKit** and a **Heavy Helmet**. Inside the locker room you can find two **MedKits**. Enter the Armory and pick up as many Weapons, Ammo, and Body Armor as you can carry.

Take a few seconds to check all your weapons to make sure they have a full load of Ammo, then exit the restroom and proceed down the hall.

CHECKPOINT: THE MONGOOSE

The crane is stuck halfway over the missile bay, so you must climb down the ladder to the base of the missile bay to leave the bunker.

Equip the dual MiniGun when you reach the bottom of the platform, and walk onto the missile bay. You confront Mangouste, the Mongoose. Kill him!

BOSS FIGHT: THE MONGOOSE

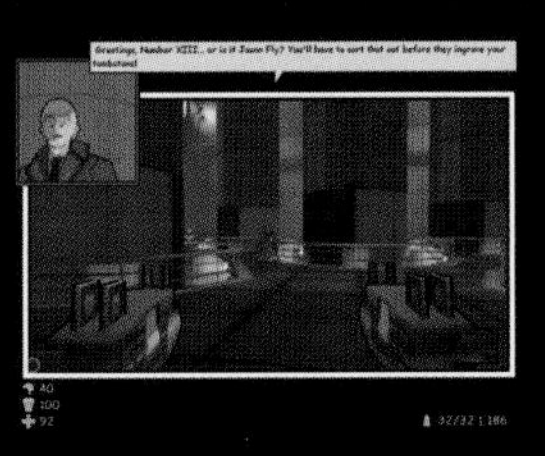

This is the toughest battle yet, XIII. Mangouste is armed with dual MiniGuns that will tear you apart.

He runs around behind the missiles after each attack to reload his weapons. You can use that to your advantage. When you shoot at a missile, coolant will spray out of the side.

Shoot at the side of the missiles where you think Mangouste is hiding. When you see him coughing, run up and let him have it!

Keep moving and use MedKits to heal in between attacks. When you run out of MiniGun ammo, switch to the Assault Rifle or M60.

As the fight drags on, the missiles lower back into their holding chambers, making it easier to target the Mongoose.

Jones will eliminate SPADS and Army soldiers on the platform above you. Run over any bodies that fall on the platform to collect extra Body Armor.

When his health is gone, Mangouste will jump off the missile platform. Is he gone for good?

Meet with Jones at the top of the platform. She leads you to General Carrington and Senator Sheridan. It's over, XIII.

MISSION COMPLETE

Mission 34:

THE PARTY

MISSION BRIEFING

OBJECTIVES

Relax, XIII. It's a party. Meet with your friends.

WEAPONS

None

ENEMIES

To Be Concluded

SUMMARY

Time for some relaxation, XIII. Join Jones and General Carrington on the yacht.

QUICK AND DIRTY

Talk to Senator Sheridan, Jones, and General Carrington. Find Wally Sheridan when the fireworks begin.

CHECKPOINT: SHERIDAN FOR PRESIDENT

Meet with Senator Sheridan at the top of the stairs, then meet with Jones and General Carrington.

Go to the front of the boat to watch the fireworks with the others. General Carrington asks you to find Wally Sheridan.

Walk down the side of the boat. You will see Senator Sheridan enter a side door. Follow him through the door and down the stairs.

Who is Senator Sheridan arguing with? Is that the Mongoose on the radio? Enter the Senator's office.

Now you remember Number I.

The end...?

MISSION COMPLETE

MULTIPLAYER XIII

PLAYSTATION 2

PlayStation 2 players will benefit from five multiplayer modes including "The Hunt" and "Power Up" with up to four players online, in addition to the two-player split-screen offline. The exclusive PS2 multiplayer mode, Power Up, is a custom Deathmatch multiplayer mode, which includes various pick-ups—some classic items are replaced with a funnier brand, such as "Frag Instant Death" (ability to kill opponent with one shot) or "SuperGnome" (character becomes deformed). Additionally, pick-ups are chosen according to the player's score position. The best player receives the worst pick-ups and vice versa.

In The Hunt, players chase a running target throughout the map. Points are scored depending on how much damage is inflicted each time the target is hit. The more often the target is hit, the smaller it becomes, so scoring becomes more difficult. Players gain extra points by killing the target, but touching it results in death!

XBOX LIVE

XBOX gamers can dive into four-player, split-screen offline multiplayer or join online battles with up to eight players. The exclusive XBOX Live mode is "Sabotage," where two teams compete to take control of different strategic points on the map. One team must defend the control points, while the other must sabotage them within a certain time limit. The defending team wins if time runs out, while the attacking team wins by destroying all of the defense points.

NINTENDO GAMECUBE

Nintendo GameCube gamers can get their fix of XIII multiplayer action with up to four-player split-screen in Deathmatch, Team Deathmatch, Capture the Flag, and Hunt modes.

PC CD-ROM

The PC version features online multiplayer action for up to eight players per map, and an exclusive map editor for gamers to create their own action-packed levels.

STANDARD MULTIPLAYER GAME TYPES

DEATHMATCH

Standard multiplayer mayhem where every player is out for himself. Frag them before they frag you!

TEAM DEATHMATCH

Team up with your friends to take down other teams of players in the Deathmatch arena.

CAPTURE THE FLAG

Help your teammates find the enemy's flag and return it to your base for points. Defend your flag at all costs from the enemy onslaught.

MULTIPLAYER HINTS & TIPS

KNOW THE MAP

Knowing where to find health, body armor, and the best weapons will make you a champion Deathmatch player on any of the available maps. Go beyond knowing just where to find the good items, and learn the best escape routes and the tricky sniper positions.

PACK HUNTING

Most successful teams hunt together in packs. While this does slightly increase the potential for a well placed Grenade or Bazooka blast to obliterate your entire team in one shot, this tactic is balanced by the increased firepower offered by an attack group.

COVER FIRE

Use high-powered cover fire from the SMG and other fully automatic weapons to distract the enemy or to hold them at bay. In combination with flash grenades, laying down a barrage of cover fire can block off an enemy's escape or attack route.

KEEP MOVING

Run, jump, walk, or crawl your way around a map, but keep moving at all times. When you stand still, you become a target for snipers.

TEAMWORK

When you're on a team, work as a team. Use your Team Chat key to devise a plan, form attack groups, and call for help. If you play Lone Wolf in a team game, you'll just be the first teammate sitting on the sidelines in a body bag.

STEALTH

Don't pass up an opportunity to eliminate an enemy with a pistol butt or knife throw if you catch someone with their back to you. This is a great way to avoid revealing your position to other players. They can't kill what they cannot see.

HIDE

When you're low on health or the bulk of your team has been eliminated, make like the mouse and run for the nearest cover. Use stealth and patience to eliminate the remaining enemies one by one or search for additional ammunition and weapons.

SITUATIONAL AWARENESS

A keen understanding of your surroundings is critical in multiplayer gameplay. An enemy may be hiding behind the open doorway you just passed. Turn and look back occasionally as you run across a map. Get in the habit of checking open doorways and keeping an eye on your back.

KNOW THE WEAPONS

Weapons inflict various degrees of damage and have different reload times. Become familiar with the differences and learn which weapons work best on each map.

HEAD SHOTS

Aim for the head. A bullet in the brain puts an enemy down quickly.

Coming Soon on PC
F.A.R. CRY
A LONG WAY FROM PARADISE...
SO YOU THOUGHT FIGHTING A GOVERNMENT CONSPIRACY WAS TOUGH? TRY YOUR LUCK IN THE TROPICS. THIS PLACE EATS PRESIDENTIAL ASSASSINS FOR LUNCH. SURVIVE THE HIDDEN EVILS OF THIS HELL ON EARTH — AND SEE WHY THEY CALL IT A "SHOOTER'S PARADISE."
weapons
humvee
mini gun
RATING PENDING
RP
CONTENT RATED BY ESRB
Visit www.esrb.org or call 1-800-771-3772 for Rating Information.
PC CD-ROM SOFTWARE
UBISOFT
© 2003 Crytek Studios. All Rights Reserved. Published by Ubisoft Entertainment. Far Cry, Ubisoft, and the Ubisoft logo are trademarks of Ubisoft Entertainment in the U.S. and/or other countries.